Principles of Accounting.com

Managerial Accounting Solutions Manual

2018-2019 Edition

Larry M. Walther
Utah State University

principlesofaccounting.com

Table of Contents

Managerial and Cost Accounting

Budgeting and Decision Making

Chapter 17 Solutions

Basic Solutions

18	**MANAGEMENT DECISIONS** Culminates in the creation of business value
6	*Planning* To decide on a course of action to reach desired outcomes
27	<u>Strategy</u> Definition of core values, mission, and objectives
1	Core values Concepts of fair play, human dignity, ethics
7	Mission Provide a focal point against which to match ideas and actions
20	Objectives Must include delivery of goods or services
31	Sustainability Development without depletion of natural resources or negative effects on the environment
25	<u>Positioning</u> Broad concept and depends on gathering and evaluating
2	Cost/volume/profit and scalability How changes in volume impact profitability
9	Global trade and transfer Research into laws about tariffs, taxes, and shipping
13	Branding/pricing/sensitivity/competition Pricing decisions must be balanced
19	<u>Budgets</u> Outline the financial plans
4	Operating Definition of the anticipated revenues and expenses
26	Capital Whether an investment can be justified
11	Financing Demonstrate why and when additional support may be needed
8	*Directing* Actions must be well coordinated and timed
16	<u>Costing</u> How costs are captured and assigned to goods and services
28	Methods Approach to capturing costs is dependent on what is being produced
3	Concepts Described as "absorption" and "direct"
29	<u>Production</u> Efficiency maximized, while seeking to achieve enhanced output
10	Inventory Popular acronyms like JIT
14	Responsibility Costs incurred and deliverables produced by circumscribed areas
5	<u>Analysis</u> Effective in stimulating correct thought
23	*Controlling* Providing leadership for the entire cost and managerial accounting functions
24	<u>Monitor</u> Establishes a logical basis for making adjustments
15	Standard costs Benchmarks against which actual productive activity is compared
22	Variances Focus on the exceptions
12	Flexible tools Compensate for the operating environment
21	<u>Scorecard</u> Draw focus on evaluating elements that are important
30	Balance Identify and focus on components of performance
17	Improvement Best practices are implemented

Today, I am very happy to announce that our search for a new ~~comptometre~~ controller has ended with the successful hiring of Bev Antilley. Bev is very experienced and holds both the CMA and ~~CFO~~ CFM designations issued by the IMA.

Bev will be invaluable in our ~~financial~~ managerial accounting function, as she focuses on our internal measurements and reporting. She has informed me that she wishes to shift our decision-making focus from one based on absorption costing theories to ~~indirect~~ direct costing methods.

And, Bev has great experience in applying ~~process~~ activity-based costing methods. This knowledge will prove especially useful given the need to adequately measure costs for our variety of products and services that are being produced in a high-overhead environment.

This paper earns a grade of 50%.

1	Billboard advertising space would be period cost, not a product cost.	
2	Beginning work in process, plus conversion costs, minus ending work in process, equals cost of goods manufactured.	X
	If you had included direct materials (plus), the equation would have been correct.	
3	Conversion costs are always the same, no matter the level of output.	X
	Conversion costs can vary with volume (e.g., the amount of direct labor).	
4	Production costs generally consist of prime costs plus manufacturing overhead.	
5	Product costs attach can also be described as "inventoriable."	
6	The cost of air filters used in the paint shop of a manufacturing facility is a period cost because they are replaced monthly.	X
	The air filter would be part of manufacturing overhead and a product cost.	
7	Nonmanufacturing costs for selling and general/administrative purposes are not part of factory overhead.	
8	Manufacturers may have three inventory categories: raw materials, finished goods, and cost of goods sold.	X
	Work-in-process is an inventory category - cost of goods sold is no longer in inventory.	
9	The cost of carbon fiber incorporated into the frame of a bicycle built by TecTrack Bikes is a product cost.	
10	Prime costs include direct labor and manufacturing overhead.	X
	Prime costs are direct material and direct labor, not overhead.	

	Total Cost	Direct Material	Direct Labor	Factory Overhead	SG&A
Synthetic rubber	$134,300	$134,300			
Lubricant - molding machine	14,000	-		$14,000	
Factory rent	9,600	-		9,600	
Electricity - molding machine	2,600	-		2,600	
Labor cost of machine operators	34,100	-	$34,100	-	
Internet sales site	1,500	-	-	-	$ 1,500
Administrative salaries	12,500	-	-	-	12,500
Depreciation of molding machine	7,400	-	-	7,400	-
Salary of factory safety inspector	3,500	-	-	3,500	-
Office rent	13,500	-	-	-	13,500
	$233,000	$134,300	$34,100	$37,100	$27,500

The prime costs are $168,400, consisting of direct labor and direct materials ($134,300 + $34,100). The conversion costs are $71,200, consisting of direct labor and factory overhead ($34,100 + $37,100).

Total manufacturing costs were $7,500,000 ($4,500,000 + $3,000,000). Of this total cost entering production, $7,200,000 was transferred to finished goods (the other $300,000 remained in work in process ($1,300,000 - $1,000,000)).

Given that finished goods inventory decreased, the total cost of goods sold was $7,275,000 ($7,200,000 transferred into finished goods + $75,000 decrease in finished goods).

Total sales equaled $9,675,000 ($7,275,000 cost of goods sold + $2,400,000 gross profit).

(a)

ASHLEY CORPORATION Schedule of Cost of Goods Manufactured For the Month Ending September 30, 20X4		
Direct materials:		
Beginning raw materials inventory, Sept. 1	$ 966,400	
Plus: Net purchases of raw materials	2,345,500	
Raw materials available	$3,311,900	
Less: Ending raw materials inventory, Sept. 30	818,200	
Raw materials transferred to production		$2,493,700
Direct labor		322,300
Factory overhead		
Indirect materials	$ 125,500	
Indirect labor	88,900	
Factory utilities and maintenance	456,000	
Factory depreciation	56,600	
Other factory related overhead	24,400	751,400
Total manufacturing costs		$3,567,400
Add: Beginning work in process inventory, Sept. 1		777,000
		$4,344,400
Less: Ending work in process, Sept. 30		717,000
Cost of goods manufactured		$3,627,400

(b)

Ashley's finished goods inventory decreased by $372,600 ($4,000,000 - $3,627,400). It is important for students to sense that less cost was transferred into finished goods (the cost of goods manufactured/$3,627,400) than was transferred out of finished goods (the cost of goods sold/$4,000,000).

(a1) 20% of the raw materials purchases remain in ending raw materials inventory. (20% X $3,000,000 = $600,000).

(a2) The total amount placed into process was $5,900,000 (($3,000,000 X 80%) + $2,000,000 + $1,500,000)). Of this amount, 25% remains in work in process inventory ($5,900,000 X 25% = $1,475,000).

(a3) The amount transferred to finished goods from work in process was $4,425,000 ($5,900,000 X 75%). Of this amount, 10% remains in finished goods inventory ($4,425,000 X 10% = $442,500).

(b1) The amount transferred to finished goods from work in process was $4,425,000 ($5,900,000 X 75%). Of this amount, 90% was allocated to cost of goods sold ($4,425,000 X 90% = $3,982,500).

(b2) The SG&A is a period cost, and is entirely charged against income during the year ($700,000).

(c) The total depreciation is $290,000 (($1,500,000 X 10%) + ($700,000 X 20%)). Of this amount, $241,250 (($1,500,000 X 10% X 75% transferred to finished goods X 90% sold) + ($700,000 X 20%)) is charged against income. The remaining amount is allocated to work in process and finished goods inventory.

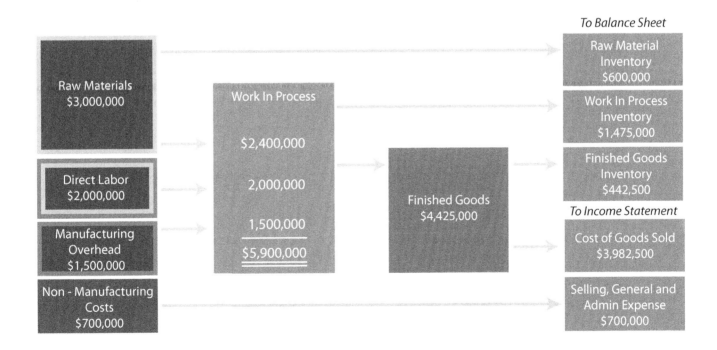

Involved Solutions

I-17.01	*Team-based crossword puzzle for managerial concepts*

Every team will have a unique puzzle. Below is a sample puzzle:

	[1]M			[2]P	[3]V							[4]P				
[1]B	2	B		R	A							E				[5]Q
	M			O		[6]F						R				U
			[2]A	C	T	I	V	I	T	Y	[3]W	I	P	[7]S	G	A
				E	A	N						O		C		L
		[8]S		S		A						D		O		I
		T		S		N								R		T
[4]C	M	A				C	[5]C	O	N	T	R	O	L	E	R	Y
		N				I								C		
[6]B	U	D	G	E	T	A	[7]M	A	N	A	G	E	R	I	A	L
		A				L								R		
		[8]R	F	I	D	[9]D								[9]D	L	
		D			[10]F	I	N	I	S	H	E	[10]D				
						R						[11]M	F	[11]G		
		[12]P	R	I	M	E		[12]I						O		
				[13]C	O	G	M							G		
			[14]C	O	S	T		A						S		

ACROSS

1 Acronym for business to business
2 ABC = ? based costing
3 This does not include that (2 acronyms)
4 Certification for management accountant
5 In charge of internal accouting minus an "L"
6 Financial planning tool
7 Focus of the back part of the book
8 Tracking chips and processors
9 Abreviation for a worker related prime cost
10 The last category of inventory
11 Abreviation for factory overhead = ? overhead
12 A name for direct material + direct labor
13 Like COGS but for manufacturing costs
14 A subset of management accounting

DOWN

1 Equipment chatting with equipment
2 Costing for continuous goods
3 Monitor these deviations
4 Not a product cost
5 Lack of this resulted in dropping the "Y"
6 External reporting focus
7 Balanced ?
8 Benchmark
9 Type of labor and material not overhead
10 Abreviation for a material related prime cost
11 Like COGM but for sold costs
12 Acronym for subject-relevant institute

	Product or Period	Direct Material Direct Labor Factory Overhead
Depreciation of machinery used in factory	Product	Factory Overhead
Commissions paid to sales force	Period	
Annual inspection of factory fire extinguishers	Product	Factory Overhead
Plastic used to mold phones	Product	Direct Material
Maureen's salary	Period	
Reprogramming of automated assembly line	Product	Factory Overhead
Salary of phone touchscreen installers	Product	Direct Labor
Depreciation of office computers	Period	
Computer chips installed in phones	Product	Direct Material
Pads used to buff and shine touchscreens	Product	Factory Overhead
Rental of mold for newest model phone	Product	Factory Overhead
Landscape service for corporate office	Period	
Salary of quality control inspectors	Product	Factory Overhead
Shipping costs for units sold	Period	

(a)

	Raw Materials	Work in Process	Finished Goods
Beginning balance	*300*	*500*	**400**
Purchases/transfers in	**900**	**700**	*600*
Transfers out/sales	**(700)**	*(600)*	**(800)**
Ending balance	**500**	**600**	**200**

The **bold** values are given within the problem, and the *italicized* amounts are "solved." Because costs are stable in this problem (e.g., $1,000 per tree), the choice of inventory method (FIFO, average, etc.) does not come into play. In addition, note the 1:1 correspondence between raw material and finished goods. Point out to your students that subsequent chapters will build upon these basic concepts to reflect alternative inventory methods and multiple raw material inputs. Point out that the "per unit" cost assigned to beginning and ending work in process may vary depending upon the stage of completion of production.

(b)

Beginning raw materials ($1,000 per table)		$ 300,000
Plus: Net purchases of raw materials		900,000
Raw materials available		$1,200,000
Less: Ending raw materials		500,000
Raw materials transferred to production		$ 700,000
Direct labor		3,300,000
Factory overhead		
Indirect materials	$ 35,000	
Indirect labor	125,000	
Factory depreciation	75,000	
Other factory related overhead	300,000	535,000
Total manufacturing costs		$4,535,000
Add: Beginning work in process		1,465,000
		$6,000,000
Less: Ending work in process		1,800,000
Cost of goods manufactured		$4,200,000

(c)

Beginning finished goods inventory	$2,800,000
Plus: Cost of goods manufactured	4,200,000
Goods available for sale	$7,000,000
Less: Ending finished goods inventory	1,400,000
Cost of goods sold	$5,600,000

(d)

Sales (800 @ $10,000)	$8,000,000
Cost of goods sold	5,600,000
Gross profit	$2,400,000
Selling, general, & administrative costs	1,150,000
Income before tax	$1,250,000
Income tax expense (35%)	437,500
Net income	$ 812,500

(a)

GRANGE CORPORATION Schedule of Cost of Goods Manufactured For the Year Ending December 31, 20X9		
Direct materials:		
Beginning raw materials inventory, Jan. 1	$ 775,090	
Plus: Net purchases of raw materials	4,334,665	
Raw materials available	$5,109,755	
Less: Ending raw materials inventory, Dec. 31	812,332	
Raw materials transferred to production		$ 4,297,423
Direct labor		3,399,674
Factory overhead		
Indirect materials ($55,080 + $320,500 - $71,715)	$ 303,865	
Indirect labor	1,232,055	
Factory utilities ($260,000 X 60%)	156,000	
Factory depreciation ($310,300 X 70%)	217,210	
Other factory overhead	77,454	1,986,584
Total manufacturing costs		$ 9,683,681
Add: Beginning work in process inventory, Jan. 1		1,213,678
		$10,897,359
Less: Ending work in process, Dec. 31		944,070
Cost of goods manufactured		$ 9,953,289

(b)

GRANGE CORPORATION Schedule of Cost of Goods Sold For the Year Ending December 31, 20X9	
Beginning finished goods inventory, Jan. 1	$ 1,242,664
Plus: Cost of goods manufactured	9,953,289
Goods available for sale	$11,195,953
Less: Ending finished goods inventory, Dec. 31	1,553,509
Cost of goods sold	$ 9,642,444

(c)

GRANGE CORPORATION Income Statement For the Year Ending December 31, 20X9		
Sales		$14,409,435
Cost of goods sold		9,642,444
Gross profit		$ 4,766,991
Operating expenses		
Selling	$1,008,660	
General & administrative*	1,073,180	
Interest expense	67,500	2,149,340
Income before income taxes		$ 2,617,651
Income taxes		863,825
Net income		$ 1,753,826

* $876,090 + ($260,000 X 40%) + ($310,300 X 30%)

Basic Solutions

Identification of cost behavior characteristics B-18.01

(a)   Property taxes on land and building

Fixed (committed)

(b)   Billboard advertising campaign

Fixed (discretionary)

(c)   Raw material used in a manufacturing process

Variable

(d)   Employee picnic with band, food, and door prizes

Mixed

(a)   Machinery depreciation is considered fixed, and the wire cost is variable.

(b)   Total variable cost for wire is $700,000. Total fixed cost for depreciation is $1,000,000 ($3,000,000/3 years).

(c)   Variable cost per unit is $28 ($700,000/25,000 units). Fixed cost per unit is $40 ($1,000,000/25,000 units).

(d)   Total variable cost for wire would be $560,000 ($28 per unit X 20,000 units). Total fixed cost would be $1,000,000, or $50 per unit ($1,000,000/20,000 units).

(e)   Total variable cost for wire would be $1,120,000 ($28 per unit X 40,000 units). Total fixed cost would be $2,000,000 (two machines), or $50 per unit ($2,000,000/40,000 units).

(f)   Machine costs would be a "step" cost. It is fixed over each increment of 25,000 units of production. Ideally, per unit costs would be minimized toward the right-most edge of each step (i.e., 25,000 units, 50,000 units, etc.).

(a)

	MILES RUN	COST
Highest Level	49	$99.00
Lowest Level	22	73.00
Difference	27	$26.00

Variable cost per mile upriver - ($26/27 miles): $0.963

	HIGH	LOW
Total Cost	$99.00	$73.00
Less: Variable Cost ($0.963 per mile X miles upriver)	47.19	21.19
Fixed Cost	$51.81	$51.81

(b)

Although the idea of charging $2.50 per mile would seem to average out about right ($1,273/516 miles = $2.47), it would not be a fair day-by-day charge. Some days would be overpriced (e.g., 50 miles @ $2.50 would recover $125 - more than the actual expected cost), and other days would be underpriced (e.g., 20 miles @ $2.50 would recover only $50 - far less that the actual expected cost). A simple and fair formula might be a $50 flat fee (for trolling time), plus $1.00 per mile upriver.

(a)

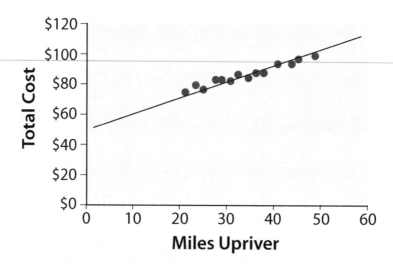

(b)

Day	Miles Upriver	Fuel Cost
1	37	$86
2	41	93
3	22	73
4	28	80
5	49	99
6	25	74
7	33	85
8	37	87
9	44	93
10	24	77
11	29	80
12	45	96
13	35	83
14	36	87
15	31	80

The regression analysis below reveals that fix costs are $51.97 and variable costs are $0.96. The R square value is near "1," indicating that the model is fairly robust.

Intercept	51.97
Slope	0.96
R square	0.97

(a)   Break-Even Point in Families = Total Fixed Costs / Contribution Margin Per Unit

166.67 families = $800,000 ÷ ($6,000 - $1,200)

167 families must be served

(b)   100 families X $6,000 = $600,000 total revenue

$600,000 - $800,000 fixed costs - (100 X $1,200 variable costs) = **$320,000 loss**

(c)   Sales for a Target Income = (Fixed Costs + Income) / Contribution Margin Ratio

$1,125,000 = ($800,000 + $100,000) ÷ ($4,800/$6,000)

(d)   New Break-Even Point in Families = Total Fixed Costs / Contribution Margin Per Unit

158.54 families = $650,000 ÷ ($6,000 - $1,200 - $700)

159 families must be served
(this approach does reduce the breakeven point)

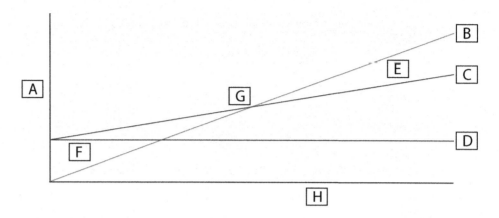

A	Dollars
B	Total sales line
C	Total cost line
D	Fixed cost line
E	Profit area
F	Loss area
G	Breakeven point
H	Volume

(a)   The contribution margin ratio is 0.6666 (($4,500,000 - $1,500,000)/$4,500,000)

Break-Even Point in Revenues = Total Fixed Costs / Contribution Margin Ratio

$3,600,000 = $2,400,000 ÷ 0.6666

The company can absorb a 20% reduction ($900,000) in sales:
(($4,500,000 - $3,600,000) ÷ $4,500,000) = 20%

(b) Committed fixed costs are generally unavoidable. Discretionary fixed costs can be reduced with adequate planning. If the company is expecting a greater than 20% reduction in volume, and desires to remain profitable, the fixed cost structure should reviewed to determine elements that might be reduced or avoided.

(a)

"Unit" Contribution = ($36 X 50%) + (3 bottles X ($6 - $1))

"Unit" Contribution = $33

Note that a "unit" consists of one lens set and 3 bottles of solution.

Break-Even Point in Units = Total Fixed Costs / Contribution Margin Per "Unit"

300,000 Units = $9,900,000 ÷ $33

Total Sales at Break-Even Level =

300,000 units X ($36 + (3 X $6)) = **$16,200,000 Total Sales to Break Even**

<u>Alternatively:</u>

	Product Sales to Total Sales Ratio (mix)		Product Contribution Margin Ratio		Weighted Average Ratio
Lens set (1 @ $36)	$36/$54	X	$18/$36	=	0.3333
Solution (3 @ $6)	$18/$54	X	$5/$6	=	<u>0.2778</u>
					0.6111

$9,900,000 ÷ 0.6111 = $16,200,000 totals sales to break even

(b)

"Unit" Contribution = ($36 X 50%) + (3 bottles X ($3 - $1))

"Unit" Contribution = $24

Break-Even Point in Units = Total Fixed Costs / Contribution Margin Per "Unit"

412,500 Units = $9,900,000 ÷ $24

✓ Costs can be segregated into fixed and variable portions.

Multiple-product firms tie sales commissions to contribution margins rather than the sales price.

✓ Multiple-product firms meet the expected product mix ratios.

Gross margins will change as costs increase under "cost plus" agreements.

✓ Linearity of costs is preserved over a relevant range.

It is impossible to increase profits without also increasing gross margin.

Per unit fixed costs will not change with volume.

✓ Inventory is constant, with the number of units produced equaling the number of units sold.

The contribution margin can be determined by subtracting per unit fixed costs from per unit sales.

✓ Revenues are constant per unit.

Involved Solutions

(a)

Variable Costs	Per Unit Cost
Feed	$150.00
Cow depreciation	125.00
Medications/vaccinations	25.00

Fixed Costs (not step)	Per Unit Cost (@ 120 cows)	Per Unit Cost (@ 140 cows)	Per Unit Cost (@ 180 cows)
Land lease	$83.33	$71.43	$55.56

Fixed Costs (step)	Per Unit Cost (@ 120 cows)	Per Unit Cost (@ 140 cows)	Per Unit Cost (@ 180 cows)
Labor (1 cowboy per 120 cows)	$200.00	$342.86	$266.67
Bull depreciation (1 bull per 30 cows)	$13.89	$14.88	$13.89

(b)

Average revenue per cow	$850
Variable costs ($150 + $125 + $25)	300
Contribution margin per cow	$550

(c) The step costs increase in increments. Particularly significant is the addition of a second cowboy once the herd size increases beyond 120 cows. This actually resulted in less profit for 140 cows than for 120 cows. The ideal operating environment is to spread fixed costs over larger units of production by operating at the "right" edge of each step. For cowboys, this would be 120 or 240 cows.

(d)

Revenues from sale of calves	$204,000
Feed	36,000
Labor (1 cowboy per 120 cows)	48,000
Cow depreciation	30,000
Bull depreciation (1 bull per 30 cows)	3,333
Medications/vaccinations	6,000
Land lease	10,000
Operating income	70,667

Doubling production more than doubled profit, as there was no additional land cost.

Team-based CVP analysis

Scenario	Sales	Total Variable Costs	Total Fixed Costs	Net Income
1	$800,000 (50,000 units)	$500,000	$180,000	$120,000
2	$700,000 (75,000 units)	425,000	100,000	175,000
3	$400,000 (40,000 units)	80,000	190,000	130,000
4	$900,000 (90,000 units)	475,000	175,000	250,000
5	$500,000 (20,000 units)	400,000	50,000	50,000

Scenario	Contribution Margin Per Unit	Break-even Point in Units
1	$800,000 - $500,000/50,000 = $6.00	$180,000/$6.00 = 30,000
2	$700,000 - $425,000/75,000 = $3.67	$100,000/$3.67 = 27,273
3	$400,000 - $80,000/40,000 = $8.00	$190,000/$8.00 = 23,750
4	$900,000 - $475,000/90,000 = $4.72	$175,000/$4.72 = 37,059
5	$500,000 - $400,000/20,000 = $5.00	$50,000/$5.00 = 10,000

Lowest break-even point in units	Scenario 5	10,000 units
Highest net income	Scenario 4	$250,000
Lowest contribution margin per unit	Scenario 2	$3.67 per unit
Highest fixed costs	Scenario 3	$190,000
Highest total variable costs	Scenario 1	$500,000

There is no single correct answer about which company is best to own. The problem is designed such that volume fluctuations significantly alter the opportunity for net income/loss. This problem should help students understand concepts of CVP and business scalability.

(a)   Break-Even Point in Sticks = Total Fixed Costs / Contribution Margin Per Unit

4,444,444 sticks = $8,000,000 ÷ (($20,000,000 - $11,000,000) ÷ 5,000,000 units)

**The company would suffer a loss if volume were reduced to 3,500,000 units
(a 30% reduction from the 5,000,000 unit level)**

(b)   Sales for a Target Income = (Fixed Costs + Income) / Contribution Margin Ratio

Note: The target income is $400,000 ($100,000 ÷ 0.25)
Note: The contribution margin ratio is 0.45 ($9,000,000 ÷ $20,000,000)

$18,666,667 = ($8,000,000 + $400,000) ÷ 0.45

Revenues need to be at least $18,666,667 to sustain the dividend policy.

(c)   Note: The revised volume is 4,000,000 sticks (80% of 5,000,000)
Note: The company needs a total contribution margin of $9,000,000 ($8,000,000 fixed costs +
$1,000,000 target income)
Note: Variable cost per unit is $2.20 ($11,000,000 ÷ 5,000,000 units)

$9,000,000 total contribution margin ÷ 4,000,000 sticks = $2.25 per unit margin

Variable Cost Per Unit ($2.20) + Per Unit Margin ($2.25) = $4.45 Sale Price

Increasing the per unit selling price can reduce the number of units sold, so the strategy may not
work as hoped.

(d)   Break-Even Point = Total Fixed Costs / Contribution Margin Ratio

Note: The revised contribution margin ratio is 0.50 (($4 - $2) ÷ $4)

$16,000,000 = $8,000,000 ÷ 0.50

$16,000,000 ÷ $4 per unit = **4,000,000 units**

(a)   Total variable costs are $27,000,000 ($45,000,000 X 60%). The contribution margin rate is 46% ($50,000,000 - $27,000,000 = $23,000,000; $23,000,000 ÷ $50,000,000 = 46%). Additional sales of $21,739,130 must be generated to recover $10,000,000 in added fixed costs ($10,000,000 ÷ 0.46).

(b)   The contribution margin rate is reduced to 36%. Total fixed costs of $18,000,000 ($45,000,000 X 40%), divided by the contribution margin ratio (0.36), is exactly $50,000,000. The break-even sales level of $50,000,000 is the anticipated revenue. As a result, the expectation is that Great Grape Juice Company will just break even.

(c)   No. Annual savings of $2,500,000 (direct labor cost reduction equal to 5% of the $50,000,000 in annual sales) will not justify the $5,000,000 of added cost.

(d)   The company is currently making $5,000,000.

Under the revised plan, total sales will equal $49,500,000 (($50,000,000 X .90) X 110%). Total variable costs will equal $24,300,000 ($27,000,000 X .90), and total fixed costs will remain at $18,000,000. The revised profit will increase to $7,200,000 ($49,500,000 - $24,300,000 - $18,000,000).

Chapter 19 Solutions

Basic Solutions

(a)

Direct materials	$13,442,769
Direct labor	21,889,554
Factory overhead	8,223,454
Total manufacturing costs	$43,555,777
Add: Beginning work in process inventory	14,550,098
	$58,105,875
Less: Ending work in process	17,559,000
Cost of goods manufactured	$40,546,875

Cost of goods manufactured is not necessarily the same as cost of goods manufactured. The cost of goods manufactured is transferred to finished goods inventory. Cost of goods sold is calculated by adding cost of goods manufactured to beginning finished goods inventory, and then subtracting the ending finished goods inventory.

(b) Alaska Launch will need a system of tracking direct material and direct labor to each job. In a manual context, this would likely occur by utilization of time sheets and material requisition forms. Time spent and materials used would be coded by job. These cost factors would then be sorted and compiled to individual job cost sheets. Overhead would be added to each job based on some predetermined rate, such as based on hours worked. Modern technology will likely be used to automate much of the cost tracking and data compilation, but the basic principles are unaffected.

Because Alaska Launch has a contract to sell at 125% of cost, it will be essential to have a proper cost tracking system. Failure to do so will render it virtually impossible to comply with the contract. Point out to your students that such contracts often entail specific agreements about "allowable" overhead items.

(a)   The job for AJF was only assigned 0.75 hours, even though 1 hour of time was worked. By the end of the day, 8 hours has been worked, and needs to be traced to either overhead (administrative time) or specific jobs (direct labor). This error would result in understating the actual cost related to AJF's job.

Information from each completed time card can be sorted onto individual job costs sheets - one for each job. The hourly wage rate will be multiplied by the hours worked for each job, and the total labor cost for each job can be thusly identified.

(b)   After correcting the error, 6.75 hours of Mary Ann's time is traced to individual jobs as direct labor. The other 1.25 hours is related to overhead. The cost of overhead is necessary (set up time, cleaning, repairs, etc.), but is difficult to match to a specific job. As a result, it is "pooled" and allocated to individual jobs based on some predetermined rate (e.g., $XX per direct labor hour). Subsequent problems reveal how to handle situations where the applied overhead and the actual overhead are not in synchronization.

(a) It appears that two valve covers were used, but the extended pricing only reflected the cost of one unit. Great care must be taken to assign the correct number of units, per unit price, and extended total cost to each job. This can be particularly challenging when units consist of "mixed quantities" (e.g., one box containing ten items). A second error relates to the circuit board. It is a costly item and should be tracked to the specific job on which it was used (not indirect material).

Errors in tracking material costs to jobs can result in lost money, poor pricing, and bad decision making. Cost data from materials requisition forms can be used to establish the basis for specific job costing. Information on the requisition form is often transferred to individual job costs sheets.

(b) After correcting the errors, $1,844 should be traced to individual jobs as direct material ($280 (2 valve covers) + $940 (circuit board) + $624 (tie rods)). Indirect materials attributable to factory overhead is only $10 ($6 + $3 + $1). Direct materials are traced to specific jobs based on job number. The cost of overhead is difficult to match to a specific job. As a result, it is "pooled" and allocated to individual jobs based on some predetermined rate (e.g., $XX per direct labor hour). Subsequent problems reveal how to handle situations where the applied overhead and the actual overhead are not in synchronization.

(a) Factory overhead would include factory depreciation, maintenance, utilities, and so forth. In addition, indirect material and indirect labor would also be considered as factory overhead. Indirect materials might include welding rods and sanding pads.

The factory overhead is applied based on direct labor hours. Direct labor hours for the Benzate job were 12, and the applied overhead cost was $360. Therefore, it appears that overhead is being applied to jobs at the rate of $30 per direct labor hour.

(b) Direct labor cost should decline, but depreciation (and perhaps utilities and maintenance) will likely increase if the process is automated. Thus, there will be more factory overhead. It is likely that the application base should be revised. Factory overhead might be applied on machine hours or some other logical basis (e.g., sheets of steel used).

(c) If the application basis is logical and volume estimates are reasonably accurate, the eventual amount of actual overhead should roughly equal the amount applied. Differences between actual and applied overhead may be taken as an increase or decrease to cost of goods sold. It is virtually impossible, and likely not cost effective, to try and identify actual factory overhead for each job. For instance, how much of a factory security guard is attributable to product A vs. product B? Or, how many kilowatts of electricity were used on product A vs. product B? As a result, accountants resort to applying overhead as discussed in the chapter.

(a) The ending work in process is $32,750 ($13,000 + $3,500 + ($13,000 X 125%)).

Direct materials	$ 11,700
Direct labor	60,900
Factory overhead (applied)	76,125
Total manufacturing costs	$148,725
Add: Beginning work in process inventory	14,400
	$163,125
Less: Ending work in process	32,750
Cost of finished paintings	$130,375

The finished jobs are assigned a total cost of $130,375.

(b) Renaissance Gallery may use the costing data to establish fair pricing for each job. In any event, it would important to know if specific jobs are profitable or not, and monitor job performance and efficiency. Costing data are important in providing managerial insight over these and related issues.

(c) If more overhead is applied than actually incurred, or vice versa, the difference is frequently credited or charged to cost of goods sold. If the deviation is large, it is a signal that the application rate may be faulty.

GENERAL JOURNAL			Page 1
Date	Accounts	Debit	Credit
8-4-X5	Raw Materials Inventory	4,000	
	Accounts Payable		4,000
	To record purchase of raw materials		
8-8-X5	Work in Process	6,600	
	Raw Materials Inventory		2,400
	Salaries Payable		3,000
	Factory Overhead		1,200
	To transfer raw materials to production, record direct labor costs on job, and apply overhead at the predetermined rate		
8-9-X5	Finished Goods Inventory	4,400	
	Work in Process		4,400
	To transfer completed units to finished goods inventory		
8-10-X5	Cash	4,000	
	Sales		4,000
	To record sale of finished awning for $4,000		
8-10-X5	Cost of Goods Sold	2,200	
	Finished Goods Inventory		2,200
	To transfer finished goods to cost of goods sold		

The Raw Materials account would contain $1,600 ($4,000 - $2,400). Work in Process would contain $2,200 ($6,600 - $4,400). Finished Goods would also contain $2,200 ($4,400 - $2,200).

GENERAL JOURNAL			
Date	Accounts	Debit	Credit
A	Work in Process	397,500	
	Raw Materials Inventory		100,000
	Salaries Payable		212,500
	Factory Overhead		85,000
	To record costs and apply overhead at the predetermined rate ($212,500 X 40% = $85,000)		
B	Work in Process	390,000	
	Raw Materials Inventory		110,000
	Salaries Payable		200,000
	Factory Overhead		80,000
	To record costs and apply overhead at the predetermined rate ($200,000 X 40% = $80,000)		
B	Cost of Goods Sold	5,000	
	Factory Overhead		5,000
	To transfer underapplied overhead to cost of goods sold		
C	Work in Process	405,000	
	Raw Materials Inventory		90,000
	Salaries Payable		225,000
	Factory Overhead		90,000
	To record costs and apply overhead at the predetermined rate ($225,000 X 40% = $90,000)		
C	Factory Overhead	5,000	
	Cost of Goods Sold		5,000
	To transfer overapplied overhead to cost of goods sold		

Six of the following eleven statements are patently false. Find the six false statements. The other statements are true. For the false statements, mark the words that make the statement false.

F   1.   With **Three** Sigma, the organization tracks and monitors "defects" in a process. Then, methods are sought to systematically eliminate the opportunity for such defects.

F   2.   A Japanese term that is associated with JIT is "**Kaizen**," which means some form of signal that a particular inventory is ready for replenishment.

T   3.   "Activity-based costing" divides production into its component processes ("activities") and more closely associates overhead with each unique process.

T   4.   Transfer pricing relates to assessing costs and setting prices for goods produced in one venue and transferred to an affiliate in another.

F   5.   "Underapplied" overhead is generally viewed as a **favorable** situation.

T   6.   The cost driver is the factor that is viewed as causing costs to be incurred within an organization.

F   7.   "Job costing" **cannot** be applied in a service business, because "jobs" only consist of things like "clients," "surgical procedures," "seat miles," "student credit hours," "fire calls," or other measures of output.

F   8.   Capacity utilization refers to the degree to which an organization's output capabilities are being **outsourced to other businesses**.

T   9.   Lean manufacturing entails the pursuit of standardization for as many processes as possible, without compromising responsiveness to customer demand.

F   10. An important part of TQM is to stress quality by comparing products and processes to other "world-class" firms. This comparative process is commonly known as **targeted marketing**.

T   11. Kaizen is a Japanese term used to describe a blitz like approach to study processes and install efficiency within an organization.

Involved Solutions

SUMMARY OF TIME SHEETS

Person	Day	Job	Direct Labor Hours	Admin Hours
Laborer #1	1	A	8	
	2	A	7	
				1
	3	A	4	
		B	4	
Laborer #2	1	A	8	
	2	B	6	
				2
	3			8
Laborer #3	1	A	5	
				3
	2	B	6	
				2
	3	B	8	

SUMMARY OF MATERIALS REQUISITIONS

Person	Day	Job	Item	Qty	Cost per Unit	Extended Cost
#1	1	A	Pistons	16	$ 400	$6,400
	3	Indirect	Gaskets	n/a	6	6
#2	1	Indirect	Lubricant	2	8	16
	2	B	Glow Plugs	4	300	1,200
		Indirect	Tape	1	7	7
#3	1	A	Manifold	2	4,000	8,000
	2	Indirect	Cleaning	1	24	24

JOB COST SHEET A

		Direct Labor			Direct Material		Applied Overhead	
		Hours	Rate	Total	Units	Total Cost	$5 per hour	Total
Day 1								
#1		8	$25	$200	16 @ $400	$ 6,400	$ 40	$ 6,640
#2		8	25	200			40	240
#3		5	25	125	2 @ $4,000	8,000	25	8,150
Day 2								
#1		7	25	175			35	210
Day 3								
#1		4	25	100		-	20	120
				$800		$14,400	$160	$15,360

JOB COST SHEET B

		Direct Labor			Direct Material		Applied Overhead	
		Hours	Rate	Total	Units	Total Cost	$5 per hour	Total
Day 2								
#2		6	$25	$150	4 @ $300	$1,200	$ 30	$1,380
#3		6	25	150			30	180
Day 3								
#1		4	25	100			20	120
#3		8	25	200		-	40	240
				$600		$1,200	$120	$1,920

If the achieved results during the three-day period are representative, the overhead application rate appears too low. The actual indirect labor and indirect materials exceeds the applied amount. Furthermore, this condition exists without taking into consideration thinks like factory overhead related to supervision, utilities, tooling, and numerous other cost components.

Comprehensive job costing (T-accounts, income statement, entries) *I-19.02*

(a)

Raw Materials			
Beg.	65,000	117,000	RM out
Purch.	112,000		
	177,000	117,000	
End	60,000		

Factory Overhead			
In. Mat.	22,000	101,250	App. OH
In. Lab.	22,500		
Depr.	21,000		
Other	35,500		
To Cogs	250		
	101,250	101,250	
End	0		

Work in Process			
Beg.	27,000	311,250	To FG
Dir. Mat.	95,000		
Dir. Lab.	135,000		
App. OH	101,250		
	358,250	311,250	
End	47,000		

Selling Expenses		
Comm.	11,250	
	11,250	0
	11,250	

Finished Goods			
Beg.	80,000	391,250	COGS
In (WIP)	311,250		
	391,250	391,250	
End	0		

General & Administrative		
Salary	56,250	
Depr.	7,000	
Other	15,000	
	78,250	0
	78,250	

Cost of Goods Sold			
From FG	391,250	250	Over OH
	391,250	250	
	391,000		

Sales			
		625,000	Sales
	0	625,000	
		625,000	

Cash

Sales	625,000	112,000	Pur. RM
		225,000	Payroll
		15,000	G&A
		35,500	OH/other
	625,000	387,500	
	237,500		

Accumulated Depreciation

		28,000	Depr.
	0	28,000	
		28,000	

Instructors Note:

You may wish to demonstrate that the total "costs" ($387,500 + $28,000 = $415,500) are reconcilable to total assigned costs, as follows:

Decrease in raw materials	$ (5,000)
Increase in work in process	20,000
Decrease in finished goods	(80,000)
Cost of goods sold	391,000
Selling	11,250
General and administrative	78,250
	$415,500

(b) Overhead was overapplied. $101,250 was applied, but only $101,000 was actually incurred. The favorable $250 variance is simply applied to reduce cost of goods sold.

(c)

HAWTHORN CORPORATION Income Statement For the Month Ending March 31, 20XX		
Sales		$625,000
Cost of goods sold		391,000
Gross profit		$234,000
Operating expenses		
Selling	$11,250	
General & administrative	78,250	89,500
Income before income taxes		$144,500
Income taxes		50,000
Net income		$ 94,500

GENERAL JOURNAL			Page 1
Date	Accounts	Debit	Credit
	Raw Materials Inventory	112,000	
	Cash		112,000
	To record purchase of raw materials		
	Work in Process	331,250	
	Raw Materials Inventory		95,000
	Cash (wages)		135,000
	Factory Overhead		101,250
	To transfer raw materials to production, record direct labor costs on job, and apply overhead at the predetermined rate		
	Finished Goods Inventory	311,250	
	Work in Process		311,250
	To transfer completed units to finished goods inventory		
	Factory Overhead	101,000	
	Raw Materials Inventory		22,000
	Cash (salaries + other)		58,000
	Accumulated Depreciation		21,000
	To record various factory overhead costs		
	Selling Expenses	11,250	
	Cash (commissions)		11,250
	To record sales commissions		

GENERAL JOURNAL			Page 2
Date	Accounts	Debit	Credit
	General & Administrative Exp.	78,250	
	Cash (salaries + other)		71,250
	Accumulated Depreciation		7,000
	To record various general and administrative costs		
	Cash	625,000	
	Sales		625,000
	To record sales of finished goods inventory		
	Cost of Goods Sold	391,250	
	Finished Goods Inventory		391,250
	To transfer finished goods to cost of goods sold		
	Factory Overhead	250	
	Cost of Goods Sold		250
	To reduce cost of goods sold for the overapplied overhead		

(a)   Factory overhead would be applied at $5.50 per sawing machine hour in the sawing department ($275,000/50,000 hours).

Factory overhead would be applied at $3.00 per direct labor hour in the polishing department ($180,000/60,000 hours).

(b)

	Sawing	Polishing	Total
Direct labor	$ 300	$1,770	$2,070
Direct materials	$ 185	$ 20	$ 205
Factory overhead (126 X $5.50)	$ 693	$ -	$ 693
Factory overhead (130 X $3.00)	$ -	$ 390	$ 390
	$1,178	$2,180	$3,358

The job was bid at $3,500 ($35 per square foot X 4' X 25'), and had a cost of $3,358. The job's price barely recovered the direct cost of production. However, be sure to note that selling, general, and administrative costs would not be included in these production costs!

(c)

	Sawing	Polishing	Total
Actual factory overhead	$290,000	$188,000	$478,000
Direct labor hours		60,500	
Sawing machine hours	44,500		
Applied overhead rate	$ 5.50	$ 3.00	
Applied overhead	$244,750	$181,500	$426,250
Underapplied overhead	$ 45,250	$ 6,500	$ 51,750

The factory overhead was underapplied by $51,750, and this unfavorable condition would be allocated to cost of goods sold. The "extra" cost was not taken into consideration in part (b), so the margin on the Washington County job is even less than first calculated. Reapplying the actual factory overhead based on the actual hours yields a revised cost of $3,500:

	Sawing	Polishing	Total
Direct labor	$ 300	$1,770	$2,070
Direct materials	$ 185	$ 20	$ 205
Factory overhead (126 X $6.52*)	$ 821	$ -	$ 821
Factory overhead (130 X $3.11**)	$ -	$ 404	$ 404
	$1,306	$2,194	$3,500

* $290,000/44,500 hours = $6.52

* $188,000/60,500 hours = $3.11

Raw Materials

beg. bal.	75,000	148,000
	175,000	
	250,000	148,000
	102,000	

Cost of Goods Sold

491,000	10,000
491,000	10,000
481,000	

Work in Process

beg. bal.	44,000	460,000
	113,000	
	160,000	
	160,000	
	477,000	460,000
	17,000	

Factory Overhead

35,000	160,000
40,000	
75,000	
10,000	
160,000	160,000
0	

Finished Goods

beg. bal.	131,000	491,000
	460,000	
	591,000	491,000
	100,000	

(a) $160,000

(b)   Overapplied, by $10,000.

(c)   Raw materials increased. Work in process and finished goods both decreased.

(d) $35,000

(e) $460,000

(a)   Costs are applied at $10.00 per $1.00 of pilot salaries. This is calculated by dividing the total non-salary costs of $1,400,000 ($450,000 + $250,000 + $630,000 + $70,000) by the pilot salaries of $140,000. As a result, Flights A, B and C are priced as follows:

	Flight A	Flight B	Flight C
Pilot salaries	$ 200	$ 350	$ 225
Allocated cost	2,000	3,500	2,250
Total cost	$2,200	$3,850	$2,475
Pricing factor of 125%	X 1.25	X 1.25	X 1.25
Price for flight	$2,750	$4,813	$3,094

(b)   Increasingly, businesses are applying "job" costing concepts to track, monitor, and price services. The concepts are as applicable to service businesses as they are to product manufacturing environments.

(c)   The costing method of Wild Country appears deficient. Fuel appears to be a direct material cost at about 20 gallons per engine hour. Likewise, depreciation is also associated with engine hours. Thus, given that these two largest cost factors are allocated based on labor dollars, there is seemingly a disconnect between costs and their drivers.

(d)   Costs are applied at $171.11 per engine hour. This is calculated by dividing the total non-salary and non-fuel costs of $770,000 ($450,000 + $250,000 + $70,000) by the engine hours (4,500). As a result, Flights A, B and C are priced as follows:

	Flight A	Flight B	Flight C
Pilot salaries	$ 200	$ 350	$ 225
Fuel cost ($7 per gallon)	420	140	1,260
Allocated cost ($171.11 per hour)	513	171	1,540
Total cost	$1,133	$ 661	$3,025
Pricing factor of 125%	X 1.25	X 1.25	X 1.25
Price for flight	$1,417	$ 826	$3,781

(e)   The prices of individual flights will be altered considerably but overall profits will not be impacted. The total of all costs will be recovered, plus the 25% markup. This would be true under either approach. However, a quick review of the above data suggests a serious disconnect between the cost of services and their true pricing. Market forces would like cause a loss of customers for the overpriced flights and excess demand for the underpriced flights. This will limit profitable growth. If the company does not adjust its costing/pricing mechanism, it should at least try to eliminate unprofitable flights and sell as many "overpriced" flights as possible. Point out that most businesses must consider complex variables in pricing, and that cost data are only one facet.

(f)   Vinita's goal would be to reduce waste and inefficiency, while improving quality and output. Many struggling organizations have seen marked improvements via a disciplined "lean" study.

(g)   Vinita's goal would be to define, measure, and eliminate virtually all opportunities for "defects." Defects could relate to paperwork processing, customer management, flight safety, and many other factors. Basically, Vinita would want an organization that is free of operational "hiccups" of any kind.

Basic Solutions

Five of the following nine statements are patently false. Find the five false statements. The other statements are true. For the false statements, mark the words that make the statement false.

F   1.   In a process costing environment involving multiple departments, **raw materials are only introduced in the first department**, but labor and overhead may occur in any department.

T   2.   The primary difference between job costing and process costing is that with process costing, costs are captured for each process or department rather than for each job.

F   3.   A job costing environment uses a *job cost sheet*, but a process costing environment uses a ***cost allocation report***.

T   4.   Process costing would be logically suited to a manufacturer of barbed wire fencing material.

F   5.   An item is **not** considered in the equivalent units calculations until it is a finished good.

F   6.   Factory overhead is **not** applied in a process costing environment.

T   7.   It would be logical to maintain a separate Work in Process ledger account for each department.

F   8.   The balance sheet of a business that uses process costing methods would include work in process and finished goods, but **not** raw materials inventory.

T   9.   Process costing can be applied on a weighted-average or FIFO basis.

Equivalent unit calculations

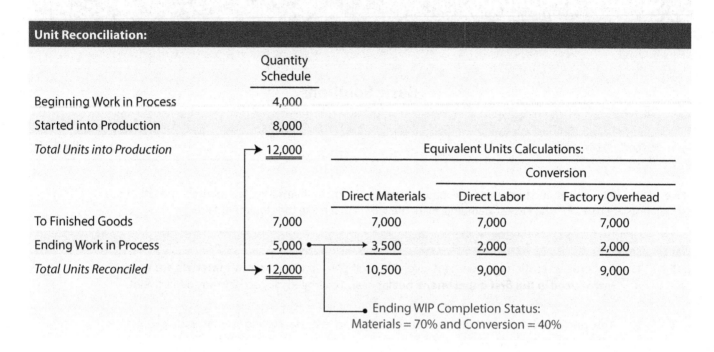

Unit Reconciliation:

	Quantity Schedule			
Beginning Work in Process	4,000			
Started into Production	8,000			
Total Units into Production	12,000	**Equivalent Units Calculations:**		
			Conversion	
		Direct Materials	Direct Labor	Factory Overhead
To Finished Goods	7,000	7,000	7,000	7,000
Ending Work in Process	5,000	3,500	2,000	2,000
Total Units Reconciled	12,000	10,500	9,000	9,000

Ending WIP Completion Status:
Materials = 70% and Conversion = 40%

Calculating cost per equivalent unit

Cost Per Equivalent Unit:

	Total Cost	Direct Materials	Conversion	
			Direct Labor	Factory Overhead
Beginning Work in Process	$ 3,000,000	$ 900,000	$600,000	$1,500,000
Cost incurred during period	9,500,000	1,425,000	2,375,000	5,700,000
Total cost	$12,500,000	$2,325,000	$2,975,000	$7,200,000
Equivalent units		÷ 9,800	÷ 9,500	÷ 9,500
Costs per equivalent unit		$237.24	$313.16	$757.89
			$1,071.05	
		$1,308.30		

Cost Allocation:

| | Total Cost | Equivalent Units: | | |
| | | Direct Materials | Conversion | |
			Direct Labor	Factory Overhead
Transferred to Finished Goods				
(8,000 units @ **$1,350.72** each)	$10,805,760	8,000	8,000	8,000
Ending Work in Process				
Incurred (Material @ **$291.35**)	$ 699,240	2,400		
Incurred (Conversion @ **$1,059.38**)	1,695,000		1,600	1,600
Total Ending Work in Process	$ 2,394,240			
Total Cost Allocation	$13,200,000			

Howorth Dental		**Cost of Production Report**
		Weighted-average method

Unit Reconciliation:

	Quantity Schedule			
Beginning Work in Process	140,000			
Started into Production	260,000			
Total Units into Production	400,000			

Equivalent Units Calculations:

		Direct Materials	Conversion	
			Direct Labor	Factory Overhead
Transferred to Finished Goods	380,000	380,000	380,000	380,000
Ending Work in Process	20,000	20,000	6,000	6,000
Total Units Reconciled	400,000	400,000	386,000	386,000

Ending WIP Completion Status:
Materials = 100% and Conversion = 30%

Cost Per Equivalent Unit:

	Total Cost	Direct Materials	Conversion	
			Direct Labor	Factory Overhead
Beginning Work in Process	£ 96,000	£ 46,200	£ 24,900	£ 24,900
Costs Incurred During Period	282,200	85,400	98,200	98,600
Total cost	£378,200	£131,600	£123,100	£123,500
Equivalent Units (from above)		÷400,000	÷386,000	÷386,000
Costs per equivalent unit		£ 0.3290	£ 0.3189	£ 0.3199

£ 0.9679

Cost Allocation:

	Total Cost	Equivalent Units (from above):		
		Direct Materials	Conversion	
			Direct Labor	Factory Overhead
Transferred to Finished Goods				
(380,000 units @ **£ 0.9679** each)	£367,787	380,000	380,000	380,000
Ending Work in Process				
Incurred (Material @ **£ 0.3290**)	£ 6,580	20,000		
Incurred (Conver. @ **£ 0.6389**)	3,833		6,000	6,000
Total Ending Work in Process	£ 10,413			
Total Cost Allocation	£378,200			

Journal entries from cost of production data

GENERAL JOURNAL			
Date	Accounts	Debit	Credit
April	Work in Process Inventory - Mill	690,000	
	Raw Materials Inventory		483,000
	Salaries Payable		138,000
	Factory Overhead		69,000
	To record material, labor, and overhead for Milling		
April	Work in Process Inventory - Sand	805,000	
	Work in Process Inventory - Mill		805,000
	To transfer completed units from Milling to Sanding ($275,000 + $690,000 - $160,000)		
April	Work in Process Inventory - Sand	400,000	
	Salaries Payable		280,000
	Factory Overhead		120,000
	To record labor and overhead for Sanding		
April	Work in Process Inventory - Cut	1,090,000	
	Work in Process Inventory - Sand		1,090,000
	To transfer completed units from Sanding to Cutting ($175,000 + $805,000 + 400,000 - $290,000)		
April	Work in Process Inventory - Cut	150,000	
	Salaries Payable		90,000
	Factory Overhead		60,000
	To record labor and overhead for Cutting		
April	Finished Goods Inventory	1,395,000	
	Work in Process Inventory - Cut		1,395,000
	To transfer completed units to finished goods ($365,000 + $1,090,000 + 150,000 - $210,000)		

	Beginning Balance	June Costs	Cost Transfers	Ending Balance
Mixing	$ 288,100	$ 1,444,424	$ (1,019,087)	$ 713,437
Blending	316,700	2,311,567	1,019,087 (3,378,909)	268,445
Bottling	454,900	954,000	3,378,909 (4,155,676)	632,133
	$ 1,059,700	$ 4,709,991	$ (4,155,676)	$ 1,614,015

(a) Blending experienced a decrease in work in process.

(b) $4,155,676 was transferred from bottling to finished goods inventory.

(c) Work in process inventory will be reported at $1,614,015.

(d) If total finished goods inventory decreased by $100,000, the cost of goods sold would equal $4,255,676 ($4,155,676 + $100,000). The selling price would be $8,511,352 (200% X $4,255,676).

Four of the following eight statements are patently false. Find the four false statements. The other statements are true. For the false statements, mark the words that make the statement false.

T 1. A simplified explanation of ABC is that it attempts to divide production into its core activities, define the costs for those activities, and then allocate those costs to products based on how much of a particular activity is needed to produce a product.

F 2. ABC **does not** maintains the traditional division between product and period costs.

T 3. ABC charges products with the costs of manufacturing and nonmanufacturing activities, and some manufacturing costs are not attached to products.

F 4. Under ABC, idle capacity is **not ~~typically isolated and~~** allocated to products and services.

F 5. ABC is **not** suitable for public reporting **(unless the effects are immaterial)**.

T 6. With ABC, the "cost objects" are broadened to include not only products/services, but other objects like customers, markets, and so on.

T 7. The first step in implementing ABC is a detailed study of all business processes and costs.

F 8. The normal steps in an ABC implementation are (1) study processes and costs, (2) identify activities, (3) identify traceable costs, (4) assign remaining costs to activities, ~~(5) apply costs to objects, and (6) determine per-activity allocation rates~~. **(5) determine per-activity allocation rates, and (6) apply costs to objects.**

Straightforward application of activity-based costing

(a)

	Units	Per Unit Cost	Total Cost
Direct material/labor	2,500 seahorses	$75	$187,500
Machine hours	1,250 hours	$30	37,500
"Set ups"	5	$2,750	13,750
Inspection	50 hours	$25	1,250
			$240,000

$240,000 ÷ 2,500 seahorses = $96 per seahorse

(b)   A traditional approach would assign $250,000 to the seahorses (($75 X 2,500 seahorses) + ($50 X 1,250 machine hours)). This yields a per unit cost of $100 per seahorse.

The traditional method results in a higher assigned cost, possibly because of the averaging of all overhead costs into a single cost pool that is allocated based only on machine hours. ABC divides the process into specific activities, with a goal of determining how much of each specific activity is consumed. In this problem, ABC produced a lower overall cost, possibly because the seahorses did not involve as many set-ups and/or inspections as did other production activities.

Involved Solutions

(a) and (b)

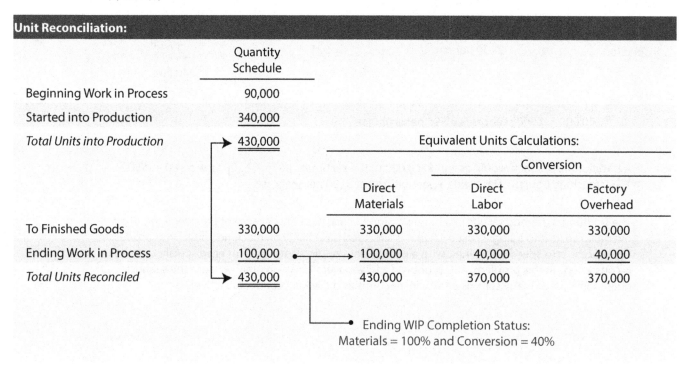

Unit Reconciliation:

	Quantity Schedule		Equivalent Units Calculations:	
				Conversion	
		Direct Materials	Direct Labor	Factory Overhead
Beginning Work in Process	90,000			
Started into Production	340,000			
Total Units into Production	430,000			
To Finished Goods	330,000	330,000	330,000	330,000
Ending Work in Process	100,000	100,000	40,000	40,000
Total Units Reconciled	430,000	430,000	370,000	370,000

Ending WIP Completion Status:
Materials = 100% and Conversion = 40%

(c) Beginning inventory included $45,000, attributable to 90,000 pounds of dog food. This is equivalent to $0.50 per pound. Because raw material costs per pound were unchanged, the additional direct material introduced into production during February was $170,000 (340,000 pounds X $0.50).

(d) 370,000 equivalent units of direct labor had an average cost of $0.25 per pound. This equates to a total $92,500 (370,000 X $0.25) of direct labor cost. Given that beginning direct labor was $20,000, this means that an additional $72,500 was attributable to February's direct labor.

(e) Factory overhead is applied at 75% of direct labor cost (e.g., $15,000 of overhead for $20,000 of direct labor).

(f) and (g)

The total cost consists of:

Direct material ($0.50 X 430,000 pounds, or $45,000 + $170,000)	$215,000
Direct labor ($0.25 X 370,000 pounds, or $20,000 + $72,500)	92,500
Factory overhead (75% X $92,500)	69,375
Total cost	$376,875

The ending work in process consists of:

Direct material ($0.50 X 100,000 pounds)	$50,000
Direct labor ($0.25 X 100,000 pounds X 40%)	10,000
Factory overhead (75% X $10,000)	7,500
Ending work in process	$67,500

The amount transferred to finished goods consists of:

Direct material ($0.50 X 330,000 pounds)	$165,000
Direct labor ($0.25 X 330,000 pounds)	82,500
Factory overhead (75% X $82,500)	61,875
Transferred to finished goods	$309,375

Be sure to note that the sum of ending work in process ($67,500) and transferred to finished goods ($309,375) is equal to the total cost ($376,875).

(h) Finished goods increased by $9,375. This means that, on a net basis, $300,000 was assigned to cost of goods sold ($309,375 - $9,375). Sales of $500,000, less $300,000 cost of goods sold, yields a gross profit of $200,000.

Process costing with journal entries

(a)

Fullerton Aggregate	**Cost of Production Report**
	Weighted-average method

Unit Reconciliation:

	Quantity Schedule			
Beginning Work in Process	75,000			
Started into Production	860,000			
Total Units into Production	935,000	Equivalent Units Calculations:		
			Conversion	
		Direct Materials	Direct Labor	Factory Overhead
Transferred to Finished Goods	875,000	875,000	875,000	875,000
Ending Work in Process	60,000	42,000	24,000	24,000
Total Units Reconciled	935,000	917,000	899,000	899,000

Ending WIP Completion Status:
Materials = 70% and Conversion = 40%

Cost Per Equivalent Unit:

			Conversion	
	Total Cost	Direct Materials	Direct Labor	Factory Overhead
Beginning Work in Process	$ 265,000	$ 106,000	$ 53,000	$106,000
Costs Incurred During Period	3,000,000	1,500,000	500,000	1,000,000
Total cost	$3,265,000	$1,606,000	$553,000	$1,106,000
Equivalent Units (from above)		÷ 917,000	÷899,000	÷ 899,000
Costs per equivalent unit		$ 1.75136	$0.61513	$ 1.23026

$3.59675

Cost Allocation:

		Equivalent Units (from above):		
			Conversion	
	Total Cost	Direct Materials	Direct Labor	Factory Overhead
Transferred to Finished Goods				
(875,000 units @ **$3.59675** each)	$3,147,154	875,000	875,000	875,000
Ending Work in Process				
Incurred (Material @ **$1.75136**)	$ 73,557	42,000		
Incurred (labor @ **$0.61513**)	14,763		24,000	
Incurred (Conver. @ **$1.23026**)	29,526			24,000
Total Ending Work in Process	$ 117,846			
Total Cost Allocation	$3,265,000			

(b)

GENERAL JOURNAL		Debit	Credit
Date	Accounts	Debit	Credit
Sept.	Work in Process Inventory	3,000,000	
	Raw Materials Inventory		1,500,000
	Salaries Payable		500,000
	Factory Overhead		1,000,000
	To record material, labor, and overhead		
Sept.	Finished Goods Inventory	3,147,154	
	Work in Process Inventory		3,147,154
	To transfer completed units to finished goods		

(a)

Vital Vitamin	Cost of Production Report
Mixing Department	Weighted-average method

Unit Reconciliation:

	Quantity Schedule			
Beginning Work in Process	100,000			
Started into Production	800,000			
Total Units into Production	900,000	Equivalent Units Calculations:		
			Conversion	
		Direct Materials	Direct Labor	Factory Overhead
Transferred to Shaping	830,000	830,000	830,000	830,000
Ending Work in Process	70,000	70,000	35,000	35,000
Total Units Reconciled	900,000	900,000	865,000	865,000

Cost Per Equivalent Unit:

	Total Cost	Direct Materials	Conversion Direct Labor	Factory Overhead
Beginning Work in Process	$ 50,000	$ 30,000	$ 10,000	$ 10,000
Costs Incurred During Period	652,500	240,000	206,250	206,250
Total Cost	$702,500	$ 270,000	$ 216,250	$ 216,250
Equivalent Units (from above)		÷ 900,000	÷ 865,000	÷ 865,000
Costs per Equivalent Unit		**$0.30000**	**$0.25000**	**$0.25000**

Cost Allocation:

		Equivalent Units (from above):		
			Conversion	
	Total Cost	Direct Materials	Direct Labor	Factory Overhead
Transferred to Shaping				
(830,000 units @ $**0.80** each)	$664,000	830,000	830,000	830,000
Ending Work in Process				
Incurred (Material @ $**0.30**)	$ 21,000	70,000		
Incurred (Conver. @ $**0.50**)	17,500		35,000	35,000
Total Ending Work in Process	$ 38,500			
Total Cost Allocation	$702,500			

(b)

Vital Vitamin — Shaping Department
Cost of Production Report — Weighted-average method

Unit Reconciliation:

	Quantity Schedule
Beginning Work in Process	80,000
Transferred from Mixing	830,000
Total Units into Production	910,000

Equivalent Units Calculations:

	Quantity Schedule	Direct Materials	Direct Labor	Factory Overhead
			Conversion	
Transferred to Packaging	860,000	860,000	860,000	860,000
Ending Work in Process	50,000	50,000	15,000	15,000
Total Units Reconciled	910,000	910,000	875,000	875,000

Cost Per Equivalent Unit:

	Total Cost	Direct Materials	Direct Labor	Factory Overhead
			Conversion	
Beginning Work in Process	$ 70,400	$ 24,000	$ 23,200	$ 23,200
Costs Transferred in from Mixing	664,000	249,000	207,500	207,500
Costs Incurred During Period	63,600	-	31,800	31,800
Total Cost	$798,000	$273,000	$262,500	$262,500
Equivalent Units (from above)		÷910,000	÷875,000	÷875,000
Costs per Equivalent Unit		**$0.30000**	**$0.30000**	**$0.30000**

Cost Allocation:

Equivalent Units (from above):

	Total Cost	Direct Materials	Direct Labor	Factory Overhead
			Conversion	
Transferred to Packaging				
(860,000 units @ **$0.90** each)	$774,000	860,000	860,000	860,000
Ending Work in Process				
Incurred (Material @ **$0.30**)	$ 15,000	50,000		
Incurred (Conver. @ **$0.60**)	9,000		15,000	15,000
Total Ending Work in Process	$ 24,000			
Total Cost Allocation	$798,000			

(c)

Vital Vitamin — Cost of Production Report
Packaging Department — Weighted-average method

Unit Reconciliation:

	Quantity Schedule
Beginning Work in Process	-
Transferred from Shaping	860,000
Total Units into Production	860,000

Equivalent Units Calculations:

	Quantity Schedule	Direct Materials	Direct Labor	Factory Overhead
Transferred to Finished Goods	840,000	840,000	840,000	840,000
Ending Work in Process	20,000	20,000	12,000	12,000
Total Units Reconciled	860,000	860,000	852,000	852,000

Cost Per Equivalent Unit:

	Total Cost	Direct Materials	Direct Labor	Factory Overhead
Beginning Work in Process	$ -	$ -	$ -	$ -
Costs Transferred in from Shaping	774,000	258,000	258,000	258,000
Costs Incurred During Period	34,080	-	17,040	17,040
Total Cost	$808,080	$258,000	$275,040	$275,040
Equivalent Units (from above)		÷860,000	÷852,000	÷852,000
Costs per Equivalent Unit		$0.30000	$0.32282	$0.32282

Cost Allocation:

Equivalent Units (from above):

	Total Cost	Direct Materials	Direct Labor	Factory Overhead
Transferred to Finished Goods				
(840,000 units @ **$0.9456** each)	$794,332	840,000	840,000	840,000
Ending Work in Process				
Incurred (Material @ **$0.30**)	$ 6,000	20,000		
Incurred (Conver. @ **$0.6456**)	7,748		12,000	12,000
Total Ending Work in Process	$ 13,748			
Total Cost Allocation	$808,080			

(d), (e), (f)

GENERAL JOURNAL			
Date	**Accounts**	**Debit**	**Credit**
Mixing	Work in Process Inventory (mix)	652,500	
	Raw Materials Inventory		240,000
	Salaries Payable		206,250
	Factory Overhead		206,250
	To record material, labor, and overhead		
Mixing	Work in Process Inventory (shape)	664,000	
	Work in Process Inventory (mix)		664,000
	To transfer units to shaping		
Shaping	Work in Process Inventory (shape)	63,600	
	Salaries Payable		31,800
	Factory Overhead		31,800
	To record labor and overhead		
Shaping	Work in Process Inventory (pack)	774,000	
	Work in Process Inventory (shape)		774,000
	To transfer units to packaging		
Packing	Work in Process Inventory (pack)	34,080	
	Salaries Payable		17,040
	Factory Overhead		17,040
	To record labor and overhead		
Packing	Finished Goods Inventory	794,332	
	Work in Process Inventory (pack)		794,332
	To transfer units to finished goods		

(a)

	A	B	C	D	E	F	G	H	I	J	K	L
			Bidding		Setup		Production		Delivery		Unallocated	
1												
2	Indirect material	$ 40,000	5%	$ 2,000	15%	$ 6,000	75%	$ 30,000	5%	$ 2,000	0%	$ -
3	Indirect labor	60,000	10%	6,000	20%	12,000	50%	30,000	20%	12,000	0%	-
4	Shop depreciation	150,000	0%	-	15%	22,500	80%	120,000	5%	7,500	0%	-
5	Shop maintenance	25,000	0%	-	40%	10,000	55%	13,750	5%	1,250	0%	-
6	Other shop costs	35,000	0%	-	60%	21,000	40%	14,000	0%	-	0%	-
7	Administrative salaries	90,000	20%	18,000	0%	-	25%	22,500	10%	9,000	45%	40,500
8	Sales salaries	55,000	95%	52,250	5%	2,750	0%	-	0%	-	0%	-
9	Transportation	20,000	30%	6,000	0%	-	0%	-	60%	12,000	10%	2,000
10				$84,250		$74,250		$230,250		$43,750		$42,500
11												
12	Units			75 bids		25 orders		2,000 cabinets		4,000 miles		
13												
14	Per Unit			$1,123.33		$2,970.00		$115.13		$10.94		
15												

(b)   The following calculations reveal the appropriate bid calculation:

Direct material	($300,000/2,000) X 50	$ 7,500.00
Direct labor	($200,000/2,000) X 50	5,000.00
Bidding	$1,123.33 X 3 bids per order	3,370.00
Set up	$2,970	2,970.00
Production	$115.13 X 50	5,756.25
Delivery	$10.94 X 60 miles	656.25
		$25,252.50
Markup rate		X 200%
Bid price		$50,505.00

Basic Solutions

1. A (~~loan application~~ / <u>budget</u>) is a detailed financial plan that quantifies future expectations and actions relative to acquiring and using resources.

2. Budgets (<u>should</u> / ~~should not~~) be used to provide managers with "preapproval" for execution of spending plans.

3. The (<u>master budget</u> / ~~sales budget~~) is a comprehensive document specifying sales targets, production activities, and financing actions.

4. "Responsibility accounting" is a concept under which managers are held accountable for transactions and events (~~beyond~~ / <u>under</u>) their direct influence and control.

5. Some entities will follow a top-down (<u>mandated</u> / ~~participative~~) approach to budgeting.

6. A deliberate effort to create "breathing room" within a budget is known as (<u>"padding the budget"</u> / ~~"aerating"~~).

7. With (~~incremental budgeting~~ / <u>zero-based budgeting</u>), each expenditure item must be justified for the new budget period.

8. The starting point for the master budget is an assessment of anticipated (<u>sales</u> / ~~production~~).

9. This comes before the other: (<u>production budget</u> / ~~materials purchases budget~~).

10. A (<u>static budget</u> / ~~flexible budget~~) is not designed to change with changes in activity level.

(a)

For each dollar of sales, 97¢ will be collected (70¢ cents in the month following the month of sale, and 27¢ in the next month (90% of the remaining 30¢ balance)).

(b)

	June	July	August	September
Estimated Sales	$3,000,000	$3,900,000	$3,510,000	
Collections:				
Prior month (70%)		$2,100,000	$2,730,000	$2,457,000
Two months prior (27%)		-	810,000	1,053,000
Cash collections		$2,100,000	$3,540,000	$3,510,000

(c)

	June	July	August	Total Receivables
Estimated Sales	$3,000,000	$3,900,000	$3,510,000	$10,410,000
Less:				
Collected in July	$2,100,000	$ -	$ -	$2,100,000
Collected in August	810,000	2,730,000	-	3,540,000
To be written off (3%)	90,000	117,000	105,300	312,300
	$3,000,000	$2,847,000	$ 105,300	$ 5,952,300
Remaining balance	$ -	$1,053,000	$3,404,700	$ 4,457,700

Spreadsheet					□□☒
fx					
A	B	C	D	E	F
1					
2		Production Budget			
3					
4		January	February	March	
5 Estimated units sold		20,000	25,000	18,000	
6 Desired ending finished goods*		10,000	7,200	8,800	
7 Total units needed		30,000	32,200	26,800	
8 Less: Beginning finished goods inventory		8,000	10,000	7,200	
9 Scheduled production		22,000	22,200	19,600	
10					
11 * 40% of following month's anticipated sales					
12					

| Sales | **Production** | Materials | Labor | Factory Overhead | Finished Goods | SG&A | Cash | Income | ◄ ► |

Spreadsheet				▢▣✕
fx				
	A	B	C	D	E
1					
2		Direct Materials Budget			
3					
4		January	February	March	
5	Scheduled production	10,000	12,000	15,000	
6					
7	Raw materials needed:				
8	Motors (1 per unit)	10,000	12,000	15,000	
9	Estimated cost per motor	$ 40.00	$ 40.00	$ 40.00	
10	Total estimated motor cost	$400,000.00	$480,000.00	$600,000.00	
11					
12	Fan blades (4 per unit)	40,000	48,000	60,000	
13	Plus: Target ending raw material*	14,400	18,000	13,200	
14	Fan blades needed	54,400	66,000	73,200	
15	Less: Target beginning raw material	12,000	14,400	18,000	
16	Fan blade purchases	42,400	51,600	55,200	
17	Estimated cost per blade	$ 3.50	$ 3.50	$ 3.50	
18	Total estimated motor blade	$148,400.00	$180,600.00	$193,200.00	
19					
20	Total estimated costs (motors + blades)	$548,400.00	$660,600.00	$793,200.00	
21					
22	* 30% of following month's anticipated needs				
23					

| Sales | Production | *Materials* | Labor | Factory Overhead | Finished Goods | SG&A | Cash | Income | ◀ | ▶ |

Anticipated cash payments:

	Units	Purchasing Activity	Total Board Feet (20 per unit)	Total Cost of Lumber ($5.80 per foot)	CASH PAYMENTS			
					Paid in Month (10%)	Paid in Month Relating to Prior Month (40%)	Paid in Month Relating to Two Months Prior (50%)	Total
January	0	800	16,000	$ 92,800	$ 9,280	$ -	$ -	$ 9,280
February	800	500	10,000	58,000	5,800	37,120	-	42,920
March	500	1,200	24,000	139,200	13,920	23,200	46,400	83,520
April	1,200	700	14,000	81,200	8,120	55,680	29,000	92,800
May	700	900	18,000	104,400	10,440	32,480	69,600	112,520
June	900	300	6,000	34,800	3,480	41,760	40,600	85,840
July	300	600	12,000	69,600	6,960	13,920	52,200	73,080
August	600	800	16,000	92,800	9,280	27,840	17,400	54,520
September	800	1,300	26,000	150,800	15,080	37,120	34,800	87,000
October	1,300	400	8,000	46,400	4,640	60,320	46,400	111,360
November	400	400	8,000	46,400	4,640	18,560	75,400	98,600
December	400	600	12,000	69,600	6,960	18,560	23,200	48,720
January	600							

Total payments exceed $100,000 in May and October. As it turns out, May is a relatively low month of production and October is a high month. This is not an unusual outcome; the cash flow does not necessarily directly correlate with monthly production. As a result, great care must be taken in planning both production and cash flow elements.

Spreadsheet ⬜◻✖

	A	B	C	D	E
1					
2		Direct Labor Budget			
3					
4		January	February	March	
5	Estimated bicycles produced	11,000	14,000	12,500	
6	X Direct labor hours per bicycle	3	3	3	
7	Total estimated labor hours	33,000	42,000	37,500	
8	X Cost per direct labor hour	$ 16.50	$ 16.50	$ 16.50	
9	Cost of direct labor	$544,500	$693,000	$618,750	
10					

Sales | Production | Materials | *Labor* | Factory Overhead | Finished Goods | SG&A | Cash | Income ◀ ▶

Spreadsheet ⬜◻✖

	A	B	C	D	E
1					
2		Factory Overhead Budget			
3					
4		January	February	March	
5	Total estimated labor hours	33,000	42,000	37,500	
6	X Variable factory overhead rate	$ 10.25	$ 10.25	$ 10.25	
7	Total variable factory overhead	$338,250	$ 430,500	$ 384,375	
8	Fixed factory overhead	110,000	110,000	110,000	
9	Total factory overhead	$448,250	$ 540,500	$ 494,375	
10	Less: Depreciation	(10,000)	(10,000)	(10,000)	
11	Cash paid for factory overhead	$438,250	$ 530,500	$ 484,375	
12					
13	Cost of direct labor	$544,500	$ 693,000	$ 618,750	
14	Cash paid for factory overhead	438,250	530,500	484,375	
15	Expected cash outflow for labor/overhead	$982,750	$1,223,500	$1,103,125	
16					

Sales | Production | Materials | Labor | *Factory Overhead* | Finished Goods | SG&A | Cash | Income ◀ ▶

Spreadsheet						
	fx					
	A	B	C	D	E	F	G
1							
2		Ending Finished Goods Inventory					
3							
4		Units		Per Unit Cost		Per Unit Total	
5	Direct material	800 pounds		$0.10		$ 80.00	
6	Direct labor	2.5 hours		$15.00		37.50	
7	Applied factory overhead	2.5 hours		$7.50		18.75	
8	Total cost per unit					$ 136.25	
9	X Units in finished goods inventory					1000	
10	Finished goods inventory					$136,250.00	
11	X Portion available for line of credit					80%	
12	Total available under line of credit					$109,000.00	
13							

| Sales | Production | Materials | Labor | Factory Overhead | *Finished Goods* | SG&A | Cash | Income | ◄ ► |

The following revised budget reflects only 45,000 (90% of the volume included in the original plan) units:

	A	B	C	D
1				
2		Selling, General, and Administrative Budget		
3		For the Year Ending December 31, 20X5		
4				
5	Estimated units sold	45,000		
6	X Per unit variable SG&A	$ 4.00		
7	Total variable SG&A	$180,000		
8	Fixed SG&A			
9	Salaries	$275,000		
10	Office	60,000		
11	Advertising	175,000		
12	Other	25,000		
13	Total fixed SG&A	$535,000		
14	Total budgeted SG&A	$715,000		
15				

Sales | Production | Materials | Labor | Factory Overhead | Finished Goods | *SG&A* | Cash | Income ◄ ►

Reducing advertising would be a "tricky" decision. While it will immediately reduce costs, it might also impact sales and corporate brand value.

As the following cash budget reveals, $207,000 will be available for a cash dividend at the end of June (the amount by which ending estimated cash exceeds $250,000). The danger associated with this plan is that the $500,000 equipment purchase must be paid for in July. Paying the dividend will leave the company significantly constrained and potentially unable to make the requisite equipment payment.

Spreadsheet						▭▢✕
		fx				
	A	B	C	D	E	F	G
1							
2			Cash Budget				
3							
4		April		May		June	
5	Beginning cash balance	$ 75,000		$214,000		$ 350,000	
6	Customer receipts	700,000		750,000		800,000	
7	Available cash	$775,000		$964,000		$1,150,000	
8	Less disbursements:						
9	Direct materials	$200,000		$222,000		$ 265,000	
10	Direct labor	245,000		265,000		300,000	
11	Factory overhead	40,000		45,000		54,000	
12	SG&A	61,000		64,000		58,000	
13	Taxes	15,000		18,000		16,000	
14	Total disbursements	$561,000		$614,000		$ 693,000	
15							
16	Ending cash balance	$214,000		$350,000		$ 457,000	
17							

| Sales | Production | Materials | Labor | Factory Overhead | Finished Goods | SG&A | *Cash* | Income | ◄ ► |

Involved Solutions

	A	B	C	D	E	F	G
			fx				
1			MILLER AUTO BODY				
2			Cash Budget				
3			For the Three Months Ending September 31, 20XX				
4		July		August		September	
5	Beginning cash balance	$ 12,500		$ 62,100		$ 11,710	
6	Plus: Customer receipts*	262,500		252,000		311,750	
7	Plus: Sale of truck	-		-		25,000	
8	Available cash	$275,000		$314,100		$348,460	
9	Less disbursements:						
10	SG&A**	$ 78,750		$ 99,000		$ 91,500	
11	Repair parts***	78,750		87,750		100,500	
12	Direct labor****	45,000		72,000		62,000	
13	Shop overhead*****	5,400		8,640		7,440	
14	Payment to Jeff in lieu of tax	5,000		5,000		5,000	
15	Equipment purchase	-		85,000		-	
16	Total disbursements	$212,900		$357,390		$266,440	
17							
18	Cash surplus/(deficit)	$ 62,100		$ (43,290)		$ 82,020	
19	Financing:						
20	Planned Borrowing	-		55,000		-	
21	Planned repayment	-		-		(55,000)	
22	Interest on repayment******	-		-		(1,100)	
23	Ending cash balance	$ 62,100		$ 11,710		$ 25,920	
24							
25	* July Collections (20% X $225,000) + (60% X $300,000) + (15% X $250,000)						
26	August Collections (20% X $360,000) + (60% X $225,000) + (15% X $300,000)						
27	September Collections (20% X $310,000) + (60% X $360,000) + (15% X $225,000)						
28	** ($70,000 - $25,000) + 15% of monthly sales						
29	*** 15% of current month's sales + 15% of prior month's sales						
30	**** Direct labor x 30% X 40%						
31	****** Interest is $55,000 X 1% X 2 months						
32							

| Sales | Production | Materials | Labor | Factory Overhead | Finished Goods | SG&A | Cash | Income | ◄ ► |

Spreadsheet ▬◻✖

	fx			
	A	B	C	D	E
1		STORM TOOLS			
2		Sales Budget			
3		For the Three Months January to March			
4		January	February	March	
5	Estimated units	20,000	25,000	25,000	
6	X Per unit sales price	$ 100	$ 100	$ 100	
7	Total estimated sales	$2,000,000	$2,500,000	$2,500,000	
8					
9		*Expected Cash Collections from Sales*			
10					
11	From current month sales*	$1,400,000	$1,750,000	$1,750,000	
12	From prior month sales**	-	600,000	750,000	
13	Cash collections from sales	$1,400,000	$2,350,000	$2,500,000	
14					
15	* 50% + (40% X 50%) = 70% of current month sales				
16	** (60% X 50%) = 30% of prior month sales				
17					

| **Sales** | Production | Materials | Labor | Factory Overhead | Finished Goods | SG&A | Cash | Income | ◄ | ► |

Spreadsheet ▬◻✖

	fx				
	A	B	C	D	E	F
1		STORM TOOLS				
2		Production Budget				
3		For the Three Months January to March				
4		January	February	March		
5	Estimated units sold	20,000	25,000	25,000		
6	Ending finished goods inventory	5,000	7,500	12,500		
7	Total units available	25,000	32,500	37,500		
8	Less: Beginning finished goods	-	5,000	7,500		
9	Scheduled production	25,000	27,500	30,000		
10						

| Sales | **Production** | Materials | Labor | Factory Overhead | Finished Goods | SG&A | Cash | Income | ◄ | ► |

Spreadsheet

	A	B	C	D	E
			fx		
1	STORM TOOLS				
2	Direct Materials Budget				
3	For the Three Months January to March				
4		January	February	March	
5	Scheduled production	25,000	27,500	30,000	
6	Plus: Target ending raw material*	6,875	7,500	8,125	
7	Total units for which material is needed	31,875	35,000	38,125	
8	Less: Target beginning raw material	-	6,875	7,500	
9	Raw materials to purchase	31,875	28,125	30,625	
10	X Estimated cost of raw material per unit	$ 40	$ 40	$ 40	
11	Cost of raw material purchases	$1,275,000	$1,125,000	$1,225,000	
12					
13	Expected Cash Payments for Materials Purchases				
14					
15	Cash payments for prior month's purchases	$ -	$1,275,000	$1,125,000	
16					
17	* 25% of following month's production				
18					

| Sales | Production | **Materials** | Labor | Factory Overhead | Finished Goods | SG&A | Cash | Income | ◀ | ▶ |

Spreadsheet

	A	B	C	D	E
			fx		
1	STORM TOOLS				
2	Direct Labor Budget				
3	For the Three Months January to March				
4		January	February	March	
5	Scheduled production	25,000	27,500	30,000	
6	X Direct labor hours per unit	1/3	1/3	1/3	
7	Total direct labor hours	8,333	9,167	10,000	
8	X Cost per direct labor hour	$ 24	$ 24	$ 24	
9	Cost of direct labor	$200,000	$220,000	$240,000	
10					

| Sales | Production | Materials | **Labor** | Factory Overhead | Finished Goods | SG&A | Cash | Income | ◀ | ▶ |

Spreadsheet 🗕 🔲 ✕

	A	B	C	D	E
		fx			
1		STORM TOOLS			
2		Factory Overhead Budget			
3		For the Three Months January to March			
4		January	February	March	
5	Direct labor hours	8,333	9,167	10,000	
6	X Variable factory overhead rate	$ 9	$ 9	$ 9	
7	Total variable factory overhead	$ 75,000	$ 82,500	$ 90,000	
8	Fixed factory overhead	25,000	25,000	25,000	
9	Total factory overhead	$100,000	$107,500	$115,000	
10	Less: Depreciation (60% of fixed overhead)	(15,000)	(15,000)	(15,000)	
11	Cash paid for factory overhead	$ 85,000	$ 92,500	$100,000	
12					

| Sales | Production | Materials | Labor | *Factory Overhead* | Finished Goods | SG&A | Cash | Income | ◀ | ▶ |

Spreadsheet 🗕 🔲 ✕

	A	B	C	D	E	F	G
		fx					
1		STORM TOOLS					
2		Ending Finished Goods Inventory					
3		March 31					
4		Units		Per Unit Cost		Per Unit Total	
5	Direct material	1		$40.00		$ 40.00	
6	Direct labor	1/3 hour		24.00		8.00	
7	Applied factory overhead	1/3 hour		11.73		3.91	
8	Total cost per unit					$ 51.91	
9	X Units in finished goods inventory					12,500	
10	Ending finished goods inventory					$648,875	
11							

| Sales | Production | Materials | Labor | Factory Overhead | *Finished Goods* | SG&A | Cash | Income | ◀ | ▶ |

Spreadsheet					□ ▢ ☒
		fx			
	A	B	C	D	E
1	STORM TOOLS				
2	Selling, General, and Administrative Budget				
3	For the Three Months January to March				
4		January	February	March	
5	Estimated sales	$2,000,000	$2,500,000	$2,500,000	
6	X Variable SG&A rate	15%	15%	15%	
7	Total variable SG&A	$ 300,000	$ 375,000	$ 375,000	
8	Fixed SG&A				
9	Salaries	$ 100,000	$ 100,000	$ 100,000	
10	Office	40,000	40,000	40,000	
11	Advertising	75,000	75,000	75,000	
12	Total fixed SG&A	$ 215,000	$ 215,000	$ 215,000	
13	Total budgeted SG&A	$ 515,000	$ 590,000	$ 590,000	
14					

| Sales | Production | Materials | Labor | Factory Overhead | Finished Goods | *SG&A* | Cash | Income | ◄ ► |

Spreadsheet				□ ◻ ☒
fx				
	A	B	C	D	E
1	STORM TOOLS				
2	Cash Budget				
3	For the Three Months January to March				
4		January	February	March	
5	Beginning cash balance	$ 500,000	$1,045,000	$1,162,750	
6	Plus: Customer receipts	1,400,000	2,350,000	2,500,000	
7	Available cash	$1,900,000	$3,395,000	$3,662,750	
8	Less disbursements:				
9	Direct materials	$ -	$1,275,000	$1,125,000	
10	Direct labor	200,000	220,000	240,000	
11	Factory overhead	85,000	92,500	100,000	
12	SG&A	515,000	590,000	590,000	
13	Total disbursements	$ 800,000	$2,177,500	$2,055,000	
14					
15	Cash surplus/(deficit)	$1,100,000	$1,217,500	$1,607,750	
16	Financing:				
17	Planned repayment	(50,000)	(50,000)	(50,000)	
18	Interest on note (1/2% of unpaid balance)	(5,000)	(4,750)	(4,500)	
19	Ending cash balance	$1,045,000	$1,162,750	$1,553,250	
20					

| Sales | Production | Materials | Labor | Factory Overhead | Finished Goods | SG&A | *Cash* | Income | ◄ | ► |

The electronic spreadsheet version of this problem includes a template based upon the existing budget as displayed within Chapter 21 of the textbook. You may find it easiest for each team member to work with this electronic template, and pass along the updated file to the next member of the team. As you do so, discuss the importance of communication between colleagues in working through the budgeting process (i.e., sales must communicate with production, etc.).

Spreadsheet   _ ▢ ✕

fx

	A	B	C	D	E	F
1	Shehadeh Movie Screens					
2	Revised Sales Budget					
3	For the Year Ending December 31, 20X9					
4		First Quarter	Second Quarter	Third Quarter	Fourth Quarter	Annual Recap
5	Estimated units	1,900	1,300	2,800	2,200	8,200
6	X Per unit sales price	$ 175	$ 175	$ 175	$ 175	$ 175
7	Total estimated sales	$332,500	$227,500	$490,000	$385,000	$1,435,000
8						
9	*Expected Cash Collections from Sales*					
10		First Quarter	Second Quarter	Third Quarter	Fourth Quarter	Annual Recap
11	From current quarter sales	$221,667	$151,667	$326,667	$256,667	
12	From prior quarter sales	100,000	110,833	75,833	163,333	
13	Cash collections from sales	$321,667	$262,500	$402,500	$420,000	$1,406,667
14						

| *Sales* | Production | Materials | Labor | Factory Overhead | Finished Goods | SG&A | Cash | Income | ◄ | ► |

Spreadsheet   _ ▢ ✕

fx

	A	B	C	D	E	F
1	Shehadeh Movie Screens					
2	Revised Production Budget					
3	For the Year Ending December 31, 20X9					
4		First Quarter	Second Quarter	Third Quarter	Fourth Quarter	Annual Recap
5	Estimated units sold	1,900	1,300	2,800	2,200	8,200
6	Desired ending finished goods	325	700	550	650	650
7	Total units needed	2,225	2,000	3,350	2,850	
8	Less: Beginning finished goods	(525)	(325)	(700)	(550)	(525)
9	Scheduled production	1,700	1,675	2,650	2,300	8,325

| Sales | *Production* | Materials | Labor | Factory Overhead | Finished Goods | SG&A | Cash | Income | ◄ | ► |

Spreadsheet ▭▢✕

	A	B	C	D	E	F
				fx		
	A	B	C	D	E	F
1			Shehadeh Movie Screens			
2			Revised Direct Materials Budget			
3			For the Year Ending December 31, 20X9			
4		First Quarter	Second Quarter	Third Quarter	Fourth Quarter	Annual Recap
5	Scheduled production	1,700	1,675	2,650	2,300	8,325
6	X Raw materials per unit (sq. ft.)	35	35	35	35	35
7	Total raw material needs (sq. ft.)	59,500	58,625	92,750	80,500	291,375
8	Plus: Target end. raw material	11,725	18,550	16,100	18,000	18,000
9	Total units needed (sq. ft.)	71,225	77,175	108,850	98,500	309,375
10	Less: Target beg. raw material	(13,650)	(11,725)	(18,550)	(16,100)	(13,650)
11	Raw material purchases (sq. ft.)	57,575	65,450	90,300	82,400	295,725
12	X Estimated cost per square ft.	$ 1.40	$ 1.40	$ 1.40	$ 1.40	n/a
13	Cost of raw material purchases	$ 80,605	$ 91,630	$126,420	$115,360	$414,015
14						
15			*Expected Cash Payments For Materials Purchases*			
16		First Quarter	Second Quarter	Third Quarter	Fourth Quarter	Annual Recap
17	From current quarter purchases	$64,484	$73,304	$101,136	$ 92,288	
18	From prior quarter purchases	15,000	16,121	18,326	25,284	
19	Cash payments for materials	$79,484	$89,425	$119,462	$117,572	$405,943
20						

| Sales | Production | **Materials** | Labor | Factory Overhead | Finished Goods | SG&A | Cash | Income | ◄ | ► |

Spreadsheet ▭▢✕

	A	B	C	D	E	F
				fx		
	A	B	C	D	E	F
1			Shehadeh Movie Screens			
2			Revised Direct Labor Budget			
3			For the Year Ending December 31, 20X9			
4		First Quarter	Second Quarter	Third Quarter	Fourth Quarter	Annual Recap
5	Scheduled production	1,700	1,675	2,650	2,300	8,325
6	X Direct labor hours per unit	3	3	3	3	3
7	Total direct labor hours	5,100	5,025	7,950	6,900	24,975
8	X Cost per direct labor hour	$ 14.00	$ 14.00	$ 14.00	$ 14.00	$ 14.00
9	Cost of direct labor	$71,400	$70,350	$111,300	$96,600	$349,650
10						

| Sales | Production | Materials | **Labor** | Factory Overhead | Finished Goods | SG&A | Cash | Income | ◄ | ► |

Spreadsheet

	A	B	C	D	E	F
1			Shehadeh Movie Screens			
2			Revised Factory Overhead Budget			
3			For the Year Ending December 31, 20X9			
4		First Quarter	Second Quarter	Third Quarter	Fourth Quarter	Annual Recap
5	Direct labor hours	5,100	5,025	7,950	6,900	24,975
6	X Variable fact. overhead rate	$ 5.00	$ 5.00	$ 5.00	$ 5.00	$ 5.00
7	Total variable fact. overhead	$25,500	$25,125	$39,750	$34,500	$124,875
8	Fixed factory overhead	53,050	53,050	57,050	57,050	220,200
9	Total factory overhead	$78,550	$78,175	$96,800	$91,550	$345,075
10	Less: Depreciation	(3,000)	(3,000)	(7,000)	(7,000)	(20,000)
11	Cash paid for factory overhead	$75,550	$75,175	$89,800	$84,550	$325,075
12						
13	The revised factory overhead allocation rate is $13.82 per direct labor hour.					
14	($345,075/24,975 = $13.8168)					
15						

Sales | Production | Materials | Labor | **Factory Overhead** | Finished Goods | SG&A | Cash | Income ◄ ►

Spreadsheet

	A	B	C	D	E	F	G
1			Shehadeh Movie Screens				
2			Revised Ending Finished Goods Inventory				
3			For the Year Ending December 31, 20X9				
4	Cost Component	Units		Per Unit Cost		Per Unit Total	
5	Direct material	35 sq. ft.		$1.40		$ 49.00	
6	Direct labor	3 hours		$14.00		42.00	
7	Applied factory overhead	3 hours		$13.82		41.45	
8	Total cost per unit					$ 132.45	
9	X Units in ending finished goods inventory					650	
10	Ending finished goods inventory					$86,093	
11							

Sales | Production | Materials | Labor | Factory Overhead | **Finished Goods** | SG&A | Cash | Income ◄ ►

Spreadsheet					⊟◻☒
			fx		
	A	B	C	D	E	F
1	Shehadeh Movie Screens					
2	Revised Selling, General, and Administrative Budget					
3	For the Year Ending December 31, 20X9					
4		First Quarter	Second Quarter	Third Quarter	Fourth Quarter	Annual Recap
5	Estimated units sold	1,900	1,300	2,800	2,200	8,200
6	X Per unit variable SG&A	$ 10	$ 10	$ 10	$ 10	$ 10
7	Total variable SG&A	$19,000	$13,000	$28,000	$22,000	$ 82,000
8	Fixed SG&A					
9	Salaries	$12,000	$12,000	$12,000	$12,000	$ 48,000
10	Office	4,000	4,000	4,000	4,000	16,000
11	Advertising	5,000	15,000	10,000	10,000	40,000
12	Other	3,000	3,000	3,000	3,000	12,000
13	Total fixed SG&A	$24,000	$34,000	$29,000	$29,000	$116,000
14	Total budgeted SG&A	$43,000	$47,000	$57,000	$51,000	$198,000
15						

| Sales | Production | Materials | Labor | Factory Overhead | Finished Goods | *SG&A* | Cash | Income | ◄ ► |

Spreadsheet						🗕🗖❌
			fx			
	A	B	C	D	E	F
1			Shehadeh Movie Screens			
2			Revised Cash Budget			
3			For the Year Ending December 31, 20X9			
4		First Quarter	Second Quarter	Third Quarter	Fourth Quarter	Annual Recap
5	Beginning cash balance	$ 50,000	$ 94,733	$ 70,283	$ 7,221	$ 50,000
6	Plus: Customer receipts	321,667	262,500	402,500	420,000	1,406,667
7	Available cash	$371,667	$357,233	$472,783	$427,221	$1,456,667
8						
9	Less disbursements:					
10	Direct materials	$ 79,484	$ 89,425	$119,462	$117,572	$ 405,943
11	Direct labor	71,400	70,350	111,300	96,600	349,650
12	Factory overhead	75,550	75,175	89,800	84,550	325,075
13	SG&A	43,000	47,000	57,000	51,000	198,000
14	Taxes	7,500	5,000	10,000	7,500	30,000
15	Equipment purchase	-	150,000	-	-	150,000
16	Total disbursements	$276,934	$436,950	$387,562	$357,222	$1,458,668
17	Cash surplus/(deficit)	$ 94,733	$ (79,717)	$ 85,221	$ 69,999	$ (2,001)
18						
19	Financing:					
20	Planned Borrowing	-	150,000	-	-	150,000
21	Planned repayment	-	-	(75,000)	(50,000)	(125,000)
22	Interest on repayment	-	-	(3,000)	(3,000)	(6,000)
23	Ending cash balance	$ 94,733	$ 70,283	$ 7,221	$ 16,999	$ 16,999
24						

| Sales | Production | Materials | Labor | Factory Overhead | Finished Goods | SG&A | *Cash* | Income | ◄ ► |

Spreadsheet					▭◻✕
			fx		
	A	B	C	D	E
1	Shehadeh Movie Screens				
2	Revised Budgeted Income Statement				
3	For the Year Ending December 31, 20X9				
4	Sales			$1,435,000	
5	Cost of goods sold				
6	Beginning finished goods	$ 68,250			
7	Cost of goods manufactured	1,102,650			
8	Goods available for sale	$1,170,900			
9	Less: Ending finished goods inventory	$ 86,093			
10	Cost of goods sold			1,084,807	
11	Gross profit			$ 350,193	
12	SG&A			198,000	
13	Income before interest and taxes			$ 152,193	
14	Interest			7,500	
15	Income before taxes			$ 144,693	
16	Income taxes			30,000	
17	Net income			$ 114,693	
18					

| Materials | Labor | Factory Overhead | Finished Goods | SG&A | Cash | *Income Statement* | Balance Sheet | ◀ ▶ |

	A	B	C	D	E	F	G
			fx				
1	Shehadeh Movie Screens						
2	Revised Budgeted Balance Sheet						
3	December 31, 20X8 and 20X9						
4		20X9			20X8		
5	**Assets**						
6	Current assets						
7	Cash	$ 16,999			$ 50,000		
8	Accounts receivable	128,333			100,000		
9	Raw materials inventory	25,200			19,110		
10	Finished goods inventory	86,093	$256,625		68,250	$237,360	
11	Property, plant, & equip.						
12	Plant and equipment	$275,000			$125,000		
13	Less: Accum. depreciation	(80,000)	195,000		(60,000)	65,000	
14	Total assets		$451,625			$302,360	
15	**Liabilities**						
16	Current liabilities						
17	Accounts payable	$ 23,072			$ 15,000		
18	Interest payable	1,500			-		
19	Notes payable	25,000	$ 49,572		-	$ 15,000	
20	Stockholders' equity						
21	Common stock	$200,000			$200,000		
22	Retained earnings	202,053	402,053		87,360	287,360	
23	Total liabilities and equity		$451,625			$302,360	
24							

| Materials | Labor | Factory Overhead | Finished Goods | SG&A | Cash | Income Statement | *Balance Sheet* | ◄ | ► |

Spreadsheet				
		fx		
	A	B	D	E
1	Oshkosh Systems			
2	Budgeted Income Statement			
3	For the Year Ending December 31, 20X4			
4	Sales		$10,000,000	
5	Cost of goods sold			
6	Beginning finished goods	$2,000,000		
7	Cost of goods manufactured	3,500,000		
8	Goods available for sale	$5,500,000		
9	Less: Ending finished goods inventory	1,500,000		
10	Cost of goods sold		4,000,000	
11	Gross profit		$ 6,000,000	
12	SG&A ($5,500,000 - $50,000)		5,450,000	
13	Income before interest and taxes		$ 550,000	
14	Interest ($300,000 - $150,000)		150,000	
15	Income before taxes		$ 400,000	
16	Income taxes (40%)		160,000	
17	Net income		$ 240,000	
18				

Materials | Labor | Factory Overhead | Finished Goods | SG&A | Cash | *Income Statement* | Balance Sheet | ◄ ►

	A	B	C	D
				fx
1	Oshkosh Systems			
2	Budgeted Balance Sheet			
3	December 31, 20X4			
4	**Assets**			
5	Current assets			
6	Cash*	$ 1,970,000		
7	Accounts receivable ($2,400,000 X 60/90)	1,600,000		
8	Raw materials inventory ($1,000,000 ÷ 2)	500,000		
9	Finished goods inventory ($3,000,000 ÷ 2)	1,500,000	$5,570,000	
10	Property, plant, & equipment			
11	Plant and equipment ($4,250,000 - $1,000,000)	$ 3,250,000		
12	Less: Accumulated depreciation**	(1,350,000)	1,900,000	
13	Total assets		$7,470,000	
14	**Liabilities**			
15	Current liabilities			
16	Accounts payable***	$ 100,000		
17	Notes payable ($4,700,000 - ($2,000,000 X 80%))	3,100,000	$3,200,000	
18	Stockholders' equity			
19	Common stock	$ 1,400,000		
20	Retained earnings $2,750,000 + ($240,000 - $120,000)	2,870,000	4,270,000	
21	Total liabilities and equity		$7,470,000	
22				
23	* Original planned cash balance		$ 700,000	
24	Reduction in interest ($150,000 net of tax @ 40%)		90,000	
25	Sale of building		700,000	
26	Loss of tax savings from depreciation ($50,000 X 40%)		(20,000)	
27	Receivables converted to cash (($2,400,000 X 30/90) - $300,000)		500,000	
28	Revised anticipated cash balance		$1,970,000	
29				
30	** ($1,700,000 - $300,000 - $50,000)			
31				
32	*** ($800,000 - ($2,000,000 X 20%) - $300,000)			
33				

| Materials | Labor | Factory Overhead | Finished Goods | SG&A | Cash | Income Statement | *Balance Sheet* | ◀ ▶ |

The proposed strategies result in a doubling of net income, improved cash position, and strengthen the overall balance sheet (e.g., equity is now > total debt).

Basic Solutions

F 1. With a ~~de~~centralized style, the top leaders make and direct most important decisions.

F 2. For profit ~~cost~~ centers, "cost overruns" are expected if they are coupled with commensurate gains in revenue and profitability.

T 3. One simple expression of ROI is operating Income divided by average assets.

T 4. Common fixed costs support the operations of more than one unit.

F 5. The flexible ~~static~~ budget responds to changes in activity.

T 6. Achievable standards are realistically within reach, and take into account normal spoilage and inefficiency.

T 7. The materials quantity variance compares the standard quantity of materials that should have been used to the actual quantity of materials used.

F 8. The labor rate variance is equal to the difference between the standard rate and actual rate, multiplied times the actual ~~standard~~ hours worked.

T 9. Variance analysis for overhead is split between variances related to variable overhead and variances related to fixed overhead.

T 10. Although a balanced scorecard approach may include target thresholds that should be met, the primary focus is on improvement.

	Sales	Operating Income	Average Assets
Segment A	$2,000,000	$100,000	$2,500,000
Segment B	3,500,000	450,000	6,000,000
Segment C	1,600,000	160,000	2,100,000

Margin (operating income ÷ sales)

Segment A	Segment B	Segment C
0.0500	0.1286	0.1000
3rd	**1st**	**2nd**

Turnover (sales ÷ average assets)

Segment A	Segment B	Segment C
0.8000	0.5833	0.7619
1st	**3rd**	**2nd**

ROI (operating income ÷ average assets)

Segment A	Segment B	Segment C
0.0400	0.0750	0.0762
3rd	**2nd**	**1st**

This problem illustrates the importance of comprehensive analysis. For example, the company with the best turnover also has the worst margin and ROI. Depending on the variable of focus, the manager could achieve different rankings of the various segments.

Total sales equaled the expected $9,000,000 level. However, the mix revealed a much higher than expected level of low margin printers (and a lower than expected level of high margin cartridges). As a result, the aggregated location margin was only $1,394,445 ($105,556 + $1,011,111 + $277,778). This margin is insufficient to cover the common fixed costs, and other costs that might be incurred at higher levels within the organization.

Spreadsheet			⊟ ⊡ ☒
	fx		
A	B	C	D
University Inn **Flexible Budget v. Actual Expense Report** **For the Month Ending October 31, 20X7**			
	Actual	Budget	Variance
Utilities*	$ 52,000	$ 54,000	$ 2,000
Laundry*	20,000	21,600	1,600
Food service*	41,000	42,000	1,000
Rent/taxes	60,000	60,000	-
Staff wages*	57,000	66,000	9,000
Management salaries	43,500	45,000	1,500
Water*	13,000	12,000	(1,000)
Maintenance	15,200	15,000	(200)
	$301,700	$315,600	$13,900

* These variable costs are 120% (96/80) of the amounts included in the static budget.

With the exception of water usage and maintenance costs, each category reflects better-than-budgeted financial performance. The flexible budget reveals that most of the "cost overruns" are attributable to increases in costs due to increases in volume. The manager should probably be congratulated for cost control rather than criticized for cost overruns.

Direct materials variances

Materials variances:

Actual Material Cost	
Actual quantity (tons)	350
Actual price	X $275
Actual cost of direct materials	$96,250

Standard Material Cost	
Output - number of monuments	600
Standard quantity of input per monument (60% of a ton)	X .6
Standard quantity of input to achieve output (tons)	360
Standard price per unit of input	X $260
Standard cost of direct materials	$93,600

Total materials variance (standard cost v. actual cost)	$ (2,650)

Materials price variance:

Standard price	$ 260
Actual price	$ (275)
	$ (15)
Actual quantity	X 350
Unfavorable materials price variance	$ (5,250)

Materials quantity variance:

Standard quantity	360
Actual quantity	(350)
	10
Standard price	X $260
Favorable materials quantity variance	$ 2,600

Labor variances:

Actual Labor Cost	
Actual hours of labor	4,900
Actual rate	X $13
Actual cost of direct labor	$63,700

Standard Labor Cost	
Output - number of clubs	2,500
Standard hours per club	X 2
Standard hours to achieve output	5,000
Standard rate per hour	X $12
Standard cost of direct labor	$60,000

Total labor variance (standard cost v. actual cost)	$ (3,700)

Labor rate variance:

Standard rate	$ 12
Actual rate	(13)
	$ (1)
Actual hours	X 4,900
Unfavorable labor rate variance	$ (4,900)

Labor efficiency variance:

Standard hours	5,000
Actual hours	(4,900)
	100
Standard rate	X $12
Favorable labor efficiency variance	$ 1,200

(a)   Variable overhead variances

Actual cost of variable overhead	$395,000
Standard hours (8,900 units X 3 hours)	26,700
Standard rate per hour (($405,000/(15 X 1,800 hours))	X $15
Standard cost of variable overhead	$400,500
Actual use at standard cost (26,900 X $15)	$403,500
Total favorable variable overhead variance ($400,500 - $395,000)	$ 5,500 **F**
Variable overhead spending variance ($403,500 - $395,000)	$ 8,500 **F**
Variable overhead efficiency variance ($400,500 - $403,500)	$ (3,000) **U**

(b)   Fixed overhead variances

Actual cost of fixed overhead	$910,000
Standard hours (8,900 units X 3 hours)	26,700
Standard rate per hour (($891,000/(15 X 1,800 hours))	X $33
Standard cost of fixed overhead	$881,100
Budgeted fixed overhead	$891,000
Total unfavorable fixed overhead variance ($881,100 - $910,000)	$ (28,900) **U**
Fixed overhead spending variance ($891,000 - $910,000)	$ (19,000) **U**
Fixed overhead volume variance ($881,100 - $891,000)	$ (9,900) **U**

GENERAL JOURNAL		Debit	Credit
Date	Accounts		
31-Mar	Raw Materials Inventory	105,000	
	Materials Price Variance		5,000
	Accounts Payable		100,000
	To record purchase of raw materials at standard price and related favorable variance		
31-Mar	Work in Process	95,000	
	Materials Quantity Variance	10,000	
	Raw Materials Inventory		105,000
	To transfer raw materials to production at standard usage rates and related unfavorable quantity variance		
31-Mar	Work in Process	132,500	
	Labor Rate Variance	10,000	
	Labor Efficiency Variance		7,500
	Wages Payable		135,000
	To increase work in process for the standard direct labor costs, and record the related rate and efficiency variances		

Involved Solutions

Team-based combined performance reports *I-22.01*

Spreadsheet			⊟◻☒
	fx		
A	B	C	D
1 Performance Report Houston For the Month Ending March 31, 20XX			
2	Actual	Budget	Variance
3 Sales	$775,000	$750,000	$ 25,000
4 Less: Variable expenses	410,750	352,500	(58,250)
5 Contribution margin	$364,250	$397,500	$ (33,250)
6 Traceable fixed costs	380,000	300,000	(80,000)
7 Location margin	$ (15,750)	$ 97,500	$ (113,250)
8			

Spreadsheet			⊟◻☒
	fx		
A	B	C	D
1 Performance Report Dubai For the Month Ending March 31, 20XX			
2	Actual	Budget	Variance
3 Sales	$1,350,000	$1,200,000	$ 150,000
4 Less: Variable expenses	580,500	504,000	(76,500)
5 Contribution margin	$ 769,500	$ 696,000	$ 73,500
6 Traceable fixed costs	585,000	575,000	(10,000)
7 Location margin	$ 184,500	$ 121,000	$ 63,500
8			

Spreadsheet ▢◻✕

	A	B _fx_	C	D
1		Performance Report Beijing For the Month Ending March 31, 20XX		
2		Actual	Budget	Variance
3	Sales	$660,000	$690,000	$ (30,000)
4	Less: Variable expenses	297,000	331,200	34,200
5	Contribution margin	$363,000	$358,800	$ 4,200
6	Traceable fixed costs	245,000	240,000	(5,000)
7	Location margin	$118,000	$118,800	$ (800)
8				

Spreadsheet ▢◻✕

	A	B _fx_	C	D	E
1		Actual Performance Report All Stores For the Month Ending March 31, 20XX			
2		Combined	Houston	Dubai	Beijing
3	Sales	$2,785,000	$775,000	$1,350,000	$660,000
4	Less: Variable expenses	1,288,250	410,750	580,500	297,000
5	Contribution margin	$1,496,750	$364,250	$ 769,500	$363,000
6	Traceable fixed costs	1,210,000	380,000	585,000	245,000
7	Location margin	$ 286,750	$ (15,750)	$ 184,500	$118,000
8	Common fixed costs	300,000			
9	Stores margin	$ (13,250)			
10					

Eliminating the Houston store would have resulted in the combined "location margin" being sufficient to cover the common fixed costs and return a small profit. Houston's contribution margin is insufficient to cover its own traceable fixed costs. This outcome was different than budgeted. An inaccurate budget resulted in unfavorable variances and a bad decision to maintain the Houston store that actually lost money.

Spreadsheet				
	fx			
	A	B	C	D	E
1	TurboTummy Flexible Expense Budget/Alternative Scenarios For a Typical Campaign				
2		2,500 units	3,000 units	3,500 units	4,000 units
3	Variable expenses				
4	TurboTummy mat	$ 50,000	$ 60,000	$ 70,000	$ 80,000
5	Shipping and handling	7,500	9,000	10,500	12,000
6	Toll-free phone	2,500	3,000	3,500	4,000
7	Credit card fees	5,000	6,000	7,000	8,000
8	Miscellaneous items	10,000	12,000	14,000	16,000
9	Total variable expenses	$ 75,000	$ 90,000	$105,000	$120,000
10	Fixed expenses				
11	TV commercial	$ 45,000	$ 45,000	$ 45,000	$ 45,000
12	Actors and models	5,000	5,000	5,000	5,000
13	Studio rental	15,000	15,000	15,000	15,000
14	Total fixed expenses	$ 65,000	$ 65,000	$ 65,000	$ 65,000
15					
16	Total expenses	$140,000	$155,000	$170,000	$185,000
17					

The variable expenses per unit are determined by dividing the given total variable costs by 2,750 units (e.g., $55,000/2,750 = $20 per unit for the mat, etc.) The per unit values are multiplied times the various outcomes (e.g., $20 per mat X 3,000 mats = $60,000, etc.).

The unit selling price would need to be at least $51.67 to breakeven at 3,000 units ($155,000/3,000 units).

(a)

Materials variances:

Actual Material Cost	
Actual gallons ($984/$24)	41
Actual price	X $24
Actual cost of direct materials	$ 984

Standard Material Cost	
Output - number of square feet painted	18,000
Standard quantity of square feet per gallon	÷ 450
Standard quantity of input to achieve output (gallons)	40
Standard price per unit of input	X $25
Standard cost of direct materials	$ 1,000

Total materials variance (standard cost v. actual cost)	$ 16	**F**

Materials price variance:

Standard price	$ 25	
Actual price	$ (24)	
	$ 1	
Actual quantity	X 41	
Favorable materials price variance	$ 41	**F**

Materials quantity variance:

Standard quantity	40	
Actual quantity	(41)	
	(1)	
Standard price	X $25	
Unfavorable materials quantity variance	$ (25)	**U**

Labor variances:

Actual Labor Cost	
Actual hours of labor	61.5
Actual rate ($1,107/61.5 hours)	X $18
Actual cost of direct labor	$1,107.00

Standard Labor Cost	
Output - number of square feet painted	18,000
Standard quantity of square feet per hour	÷ 300
Standard hours to achieve output	60
Standard rate per hour	X $17
Standard cost of direct labor	$1,020.00

Total labor variance (standard cost v. actual cost)	$ (87.00) **U**

Labor rate variance:

Standard rate	$ 17.00
Actual rate	(18.00)
	$ (1.00)
Actual hours	61.5
Unfavorable labor rate variance	$ (61.50) **U**

Labor efficiency variance:

Standard hours	60
Actual hours	(61.5)
	(1.5)
Standard rate	X $17.00
Unfavorable labor efficiency variance	$ (25.50) **U**

(b)

GENERAL JOURNAL				
Date	**Accounts**		**Debit**	**Credit**
	Raw Materials Inventory		1,025.00	
	Materials Price Variance			41.00
	Accounts Payable			984.00
	To record purchase of raw materials at standard price and related favorable variance			
	Work in Process		1,000.00	
	Materials Quantity Variance		25.00	
	Raw Materials Inventory			1,025.00
	To transfer raw materials to production at standard usage rates and related unfavorable quantity variance			
	Work in Process		1,020.00	
	Labor Rate Variance		61.50	
	Labor Efficiency Variance		25.50	
	Wages Payable			1,107.00
	To increase work in process for the standard direct labor costs, and record the related rate and efficiency variances			

(a)   Variable overhead variances

Actual cost of variable overhead	$250,000

Standard hours (30,000 books ÷ 100 per hour)	300
Standard rate per hour	X $800
Standard cost of variable overhead	$240,000

Actual use at standard cost (310 hours X $800)	$248,000

Total variable overhead variance ($240,000 - $250,000)	$ (10,000)	**U**
Variable overhead spending variance ($248,000 - $250,000)	$ (2,000)	**U**
Variable overhead efficiency variance ($240,000 - $248,000)	$ (8,000)	**U**

Fixed overhead variances

Actual cost of fixed overhead	$120,000

Standard hours	300
Standard rate per hour	X $450
Standard cost of fixed overhead	$135,000

Budgeted fixed overhead ($450 X (28,000 books ÷ 100 per hour))	$126,000

Total fixed overhead variance ($135,000 - $120,000)	$ 15,000	**F**
Fixed overhead spending variance ($126,000 - $120,000)	$ 6,000	**F**
Fixed overhead volume variance ($135,000 - $126,000)	$ 9,000	**F**

(b)

GENERAL JOURNAL			
Date	**Accounts**	**Debit**	**Credit**
	Work in Process	240,000	
	Variable Overhead Spending Variance	2,000	
	Variable Overhead Efficiency Variance	8,000	
	Factory Overhead		250,000
	To increase work in process for the standard variable overhead, and record the related spending and efficiency variances		
	Work in Process	135,000	
	Fixed Overhead Spending Variance		6,000
	Fixed Overhead Volume Variance		9,000
	Factory Overhead		120,000
	To increase work in process for the standard fixed overhead, and record the related spending and volume variances		

✓   A favorable materials price variance is recorded with a credit.

The "actual price" is used in calculating the materials quantity variance.

When the standard hourly rate is greater than the actual hourly rate, a favorable labor efficiency variance results.

✓   The net (or sum) of the labor rate and labor efficiency variances will also equal the difference between the actual labor cost and the standard labor hours at the standard labor rate.

By definition, the variable overhead volume variance is always zero.

✓   The variable overhead efficiency variance can really be a reflection of the efficiency of the application base, rather than overhead spending/consumption itself.

✓   If actual fixed overhead is less than budgeted fixed overhead, a favorable fixed overhead spending variance results.

When fixed overhead variances are recorded in the journal, Work in Process is debited for the budgeted fixed overhead amount.

Basic Solutions

	Variable Costing	*Absorption Costing*
Generally accepted accounting principles require this method for external reporting.		✓
Includes fixed manufacturing costs as a product cost.		✓
Variable SG&A is treated as a period cost.	✓	✓
The cost assigned to ending inventory would be less under which method?	✓	
Increases in inventory will cause income to be higher under which method?		✓
Results in a measurable value known as "gross profit."		✓
Results in a measurable value known as "contribution margin."	✓	
Factory depreciation is allocated to inventory.		✓
Variable factory overhead is allocated to inventory.	✓	✓

Absorption Costing

Variable manufacturing costs ($0.80 X 650,000)	$ 520,000
Fixed manufacturing costs	1,450,000
Cost of goods manufactured	$1,970,000
Cost of goods sold ($1,970,000 X (620,000/650,000))	1,879,077
Ending inventory ($1,970,000 X (30,000/650,000))	$ 90,923

Sales (620,000 X $4.40)		$2,728,000
Cost of goods sold		1,879,077
Gross profit		$ 848,923
Selling, general, & administrative costs		
Variable (620,000 X $0.90)	$558,000	
Fixed	235,000	793,000
Net income		$ 55,923

Variable Costing

Ending inventory ($0.80 X 30,000)	$ 24,000

Sales (620,000 X $4.40)		$2,728,000
Variable manufacturing costs ($0.80 X 620,000)		496,000
Variable manufacturing margin		$2,232,000
Variable SG&A (620,000 X $0.90)		558,000
Contribution margin		$1,674,000
Fixed expenses		
Manufacturing	$1,450,000	
SG&A	235,000	1,685,000
Net income		$ (11,000)

Note that the difference in income between the two methods, for this first year of operation, is also the difference in ending inventory. Also discuss why income is positive under absorption costing and negative under variable costing.

Absorption Costing		
Sales (9,000 X $5,000) + (1,000 X $4,000)		$49,000,000
Cost of goods sold		42,000,000
Gross profit		$ 7,000,000
Selling, general, & administrative costs		
Variable (10,000 X $100)	$ 1,000,000	
Fixed	5,800,000	6,800,000
Net income		$ 200,000

Variable Costing (9,000 units)		
Sales (9,000 X $5,000)		$45,000,000
Variable manufacturing costs (9,000 X $3,000)		27,000,000
Variable manufacturing margin		$18,000,000
Variable SG&A (9,000 X $100)		900,000
Contribution margin		$17,100,000
Fixed expenses		
Manufacturing	$12,000,000	
SG&A	5,800,000	17,800,000
Net income		$ (700,000)

Variable Costing (10,000 units)		
Sales (9,000 X $5,000) + (1,000 X $4,000)		$49,000,000
Variable manufacturing costs (10,000 X $3,000)		30,000,000
Variable manufacturing margin		$19,000,000
Variable SG&A (10,000 X $100)		1,000,000
Contribution margin		$18,000,000
Fixed expenses		
Manufacturing	$12,000,000	
SG&A	5,800,000	17,800,000
Net income		$ 200,000

Under absorption costing, net income decreases by accepting the special order. The company's profit decreases from $500,000 to $200,000. Under variable costing, the company goes from a loss of $700,000 to a profit of $200,000. Note that the profit is the same under both methods when there is not beginning or ending inventory.

The essential difference is that fixed manufacturing overhead is all charged to expense under variable costing, but is partially carried as an asset in inventory under absorption costing. There is no single right answer as to whether the order should be accepted. The key point is to think critically about cost allocations, and how they can influence the decision-making logic that should be applied.

(a) These are subtracted from the segment margin to arrive at net income.

General corporate costs

(b) This amount is useful in evaluating management performance for a unit.

Controllable contribution margin

(c) This is the result of subtracting all variable costs from revenues.

Contribution margin

(d) This is a measure of business viability.

Segment margin

(e) This result would not relate to any segment, but only the corporate total.

Net income

(f) These are incurred by a unit, but are not useful in evaluating unit management.

Uncontrollable fixed costs

(g) These costs may be attributable to a division, but not a specific product.

Non-traceable

(h) This amount is subtracted from the contribution margin to find the controllable contribution margin.

Controllable fixed costs

20X4 Divisional Report for Sugar Products Contribution Income Statement	
Sales	$45,750,000
Less:	
Variable product costs	21,700,000
Variable selling, general, and administrative costs	9,050,000
Total variable costs	$30,750,000
Contribution margin	15,000,000
Less: Controllable fixed costs ($10,250,000 + $1,500,000)	11,750,000
Controllable contribution margin	$ 3,250,000
Less: Uncontrollable fixed costs ($3,600,000 + $1,750,000)	5,350,000
Segment margin	$ (2,100,000)

If the manager is evaluated on controllable contribution margin, then a profit is evident. However, great care must be taken in this evaluation as there are other costs that are incurred in the operation. The total segment margin is negative, and this number does not yet include consideration of general corporate expenses.

Capital expenditures	✓
Contribution margin	
Controllable contribution margin	
Depreciation and amortization	✓
Major customers	✓
Net sales	✓
Operating income	✓
Reconciliation of total segment income to corporate income	✓
Residual income	
Sales by global geographic area	✓
Total assets	✓
Total variable costs	

Residual income   *B-23.07*

(a)

	Paint segment	Wallpaper segment	Tools segment
Segment operating income	$650,000	$475,000	$900,000
Less: Assumed cost of capital			
$6,500,000 X 10%	650,000		
$3,500,000 X 10%		350,000	
$7,500,000 X 10%	-	-	750,000
Residual income	$ -	$125,000	$150,000

The tools segment has the highest residual income.

(b)

	Paint segment	Wallpaper segment	Tools segment
Segment operating income	$650,000	$475,000	$900,000
Less: Assumed cost of capital			
$6,500,000 X 5%	325,000		
$3,500,000 X 5%		175,000	
$7,500,000 X 5%	-	-	375,000
Residual income	$325,000	$300,000	$525,000

The tools segment still has the highest residual income, but paint has now surpassed wallpaper.

(a)

	Health clinic	Janitorial service	Cutting department	Laminating department
Cost incurred	$ 180,000	$ 125,000	$ 700,000	$ 800,000
Clinic allocation	(180,000)	-	72,000	108,000
Janitorial allocation	-	(125,000)	75,000	50,000
Total cost	$ -	$ -	$ 847,000	$ 958,000

Clinic allocations:

To cutting = $180,000 X (10/(10 + 15))

To laminating = $180,000 X (15/(10 + 15))

Janitorial allocations:

To cutting = $125,000 X (12,000/(12,000 + 8,000))

To laminating = $125,000 X (8,000/(12,000 + 8,000))

(b)

	Health clinic	Janitorial service	Cutting department	Laminating department
Cost incurred	$ 180,000	$ 125,000	$ 700,000	$ 800,000
Clinic allocation	(180,000)	24,828	62,069	93,103
Janitorial allocation	-	(149,828)	89,897	59,931
Total cost	$ -	$ -	$ 851,966	$ 953,035

Clinic allocations:

To janitorial = $180,000 X (4/(4 + 10 + 15))

To cutting = $180,000 X (10/(4 + 10 + 15))

To laminating = $180,000 X (15/(4 + 10 + 15))

Janitorial allocations:

To cutting = $149,828 X (12,000/(12,000 + 8,000))

To laminating = $149,828 X (8,000/(12,000 + 8,000))

Involved Solutions

Variable and absorption costing   *I-23.01*

(a)
Ending inventory contained 5,000 units. Simply, inventory increased by 2,000 units (22,000 produced - 20,000 sold). The beginning inventory of 3,000 units, plus the 2,000 unit increase, yields an ending inventory of 5,000 units.

Under variable costing, the ending inventory would contain only the variable manufacturing costs ($150 + $100 + $75 = $325 per unit). 5,000 units X $325 = $1,625,000 ending inventory.

Under absorption costing, the ending inventory would contain the variable manufacturing costs ($325 per unit) plus allocated fixed manufacturing overhead ($242,000/22,000 units = $11 per unit). 5,000 units X ($325 + $11) = $1,680,000 ending inventory.

(b)

Sales (20,000 X $600)		$12,000,000
Variable manufacturing costs (20,000 X $325)		6,500,000
Variable manufacturing margin		$ 5,500,000
Variable SG&A (20,000 X $50)		1,000,000
Contribution margin		$ 4,500,000
Fixed expenses		
Manufacturing	$ 242,000	
SG&A	1,450,000	1,692,000
Net income		$ 2,808,000

(c)

Sales (20,000 X $600)		$12,000,000
Cost of goods sold (20,000 X ($325 + $11))		6,720,000
Gross profit		$ 5,280,000
Selling, general, & administrative costs		
Variable SG&A (20,000 X $50)	$1,000,000	
Fixed	1,450,000	2,450,000
Net income		$ 2,830,000

(d)
The per unit cost assigned to beginning and ending inventory is unlikely to be the same. Costs tend to change over time. Even if costs are stable, the amount assigned to inventory can vary considerably with absorption costing. This occurs because the fixed manufacturing cost is assigned to the units produced; fluctuations in production volume therefore bring about a change in per unit cost.

(a)

Contribution Income Statements			
	SD	CF	MS
Sales	$4,400,000	$3,000,000	$12,960,000
Less:			
Variable product costs	$3,000,000	$1,800,000	$10,800,000
Variable selling costs	308,000	-	1,800,000
Total variable costs	$3,308,000	$1,800,000	$12,600,000
Contribution margin	$1,092,000	$1,200,000	$ 360,000
Less: Controllable fixed costs	-	290,000	250,000
Controllable contribution margin	$1,092,000	$ 910,000	$ 110,000
Less: Uncontrollable fixed costs	175,000	180,000	166,000
Segment margin	$ 917,000	$ 730,000	$ (56,000)

(b)

Combined Contribution Income Statements	
Sales	$20,360,000
Less:	
Variable product costs	$15,600,000
Variable selling costs	2,108,000
Total variable costs	$17,708,000
Contribution margin	$ 2,652,000
Less: Controllable fixed costs	540,000
Controllable contribution margin	$ 2,112,000
Less: Uncontrollable fixed costs	521,000
Segment margin	$ 1,591,000
Less: General corporate expenses	275,000
Net income	$ 1,316,000

(c)
The company, overall, appears to be performing successfully. However, the segmented data reveals that MS has a negative segment margin, despite its much higher overall sales.

Below is a revision of the monthly operating report to reflect the elimination of appliances. Television sales and variable expenses are each increased by 40%. $115,000 of the appliance unit's fixed costs are transferred to TVs.

	Total	Computers	TVs	~~Appliances~~
Sales	$2,430,000	$750,000	$1,680,000	$ -
Variable expenses	2,000,000	600,000	1,400,000	-
Contribution margin	$ 430,000	$150,000	$ 280,000	$ -
Fixed expenses	295,000	100,000	195,000	-
Income (loss)	$ 135,000	$ 50,000	$ 85,000	$ -

Note that eliminating appliance sales results in a decrease in overall profitability. Fixed costs of $115,000 continue, and the additional margin from selling more TVs is not sufficient to offset the loss of contribution margin that was being generated from appliances. Great care is needed to make good decisions about eliminating product lines.

Direct Allocation:

	Mainten-ance	Food services	Information technology	Design	Printing	Binding	Ware-housing
Cost incurred	$ 225,000	$ 260,000	$ 190,000	$400,000	$1,800,000	$650,000	$180,000
Maintenance	(225,000)	-	-	26,471	66,176	33,088	99,265
Food Services	-	(260,000)	-	57,778	115,556	43,333	43,333
IT	-	-	(190,000)	57,000	85,500	19,000	28,500
Total cost	$ -	$ -	$ -	$541,248	$2,067,232	$745,422	$351,098

Maintenance allocations:

To design = $225,000 X (2,400/(2,400 + 6,000 + 3,000 + 9,000))

To printing = $225,000 X (6,000/(2,400 + 6,000 + 3,000 + 9,000))

To binding = $225,000 X (3,000/(2,400 + 6,000 + 3,000 + 9,000))

To warehousing = $225,000 X (9,000/(2,400 + 6,000 + 3,000 + 9,000))

Food services allocations:

To design = $260,000 X (4/(4 + 8 + 3 + 3))

To printing = $260,000 X (8/(4 + 8 + 3 + 3))

To binding = $260,000 X (3/(4 + 8 + 3 + 3))

To warehousing = $260,000 X (3/(4 + 8 + 3 + 3))

IT allocations:

To design = $190,000 X (6/(6 + 9 + 2 + 3))

To printing = $190,000 X (9/(6 + 9 + 2 + 3))

To binding = $190,000 X (2/(6 + 9 + 2 + 3))

To warehousing = $190,000 X (3/(6 + 9 + 2 + 3))

Step Allocation:

	Mainten-ance	Food services	Information technology	Design	Printing	Binding	Ware-housing
Cost incurred	$ 225,000	$ 260,000	$ 190,000	$400,000	$1,800,000	$650,000	$180,000
Maintenance	(225,000)	27,664	9,221	22,131	55,328	27,664	82,992
Food services	-	(287,664)	41,095	54,793	109,586	41,095	41,095
IT	-	-	(240,316)	72,095	108,142	24,032	36,047
Total cost	$ -	$ -	$ -	$549,019	$2,073,056	$742,790	$340,134

Maintenance allocations:

To food services = $225,000 X (3,000/(3,000 + 1,000 + 2,400 + 6,000 + 3,000 + 9,000))

To IT = $225,000 X (1,000/(3,000 + 1,000 + 2,400 + 6,000 + 3,000 + 9,000))

To design = $225,000 X (2,400/(3,000 + 1,000 + 2,400 + 6,000 + 3,000 + 9,000))

To printing = $225,000 X (6,000/(3,000 + 1,000 + 2,400 + 6,000 + 3,000 + 9,000))

To binding = $225,000 X (3,000/(3,000 + 1,000 + 2,400 + 6,000 + 3,000 + 9,000))

To warehousing = $225,000 X (9,000/(3,000 + 1,000 + 2,400 + 6,000 + 3,000 + 9,000))

Food services allocations:

To IT = $287,664 X (3/(3 + 4 + 8 + 3 + 3))

To design = $287,664 X (4/(3 + 4 + 8 + 3 + 3))

To printing = $287,664 X (8/(3 + 4 + 8 + 3 + 3))

To binding = $287,664 X (3/(3 + 4 + 8 + 3 + 3))

To warehousing = $287,664 X (3/(3 + 4 + 8 + 3 + 3))

IT allocations:

To design = $240,316 X (6/(6 + 9 + 2 + 3))

To printing = $240,316 X (9/(6 + 9 + 2 + 3))

To binding = $240,316 X (2/(6 + 9 + 2 + 3))

To warehousing = $240,316 X (3/(6 + 9 + 2 + 3))

(a)   David is the most expensive, at $2,771.52

(b)   Tuition is the largest cost, at $2,315.00.

(c)   Modern information systems permit easy mining of vast arrays of data. This enables detailed examined of costs and revenues, sorted many different ways. Management is thereby able to quickly and efficiently pinpoint areas of strength and weakness.

(d)   Below is a pivot table that includes data from the problem. With a bit of clicking, you should be able to verify the solutions to part (a) and part (b), as well experiment with numerous other sorts of the tabular information.

Pivot Table					
	Data				
Expense	Sum of Cathy	Sum of David	Sum of Rachel	Sum of Caroline	Sum of Total
Auto	$ 220.20	$ -	$ 124.44	$ 188.88	$ 533.52
Books	332.23	433.89	779.54	210.00	1,755.66
Clothing	66.90	423.65	103.19	385.58	979.32
Electricity	68.90	110.78	55.89	76.99	312.56
Entertainment	44.67	25.00	321.56	66.56	457.79
Food	150.76	344.56	266.76	222.92	985.00
Insurance	87.76	55.55	144.09	47.75	335.15
Phone	45.45	88.09	25.00	37.98	196.52
Rent	475.00	300.00	395.00	225.00	1,395.00
Tuition	825.00	990.00	-	500.00	2,315.00
Grand Total	$2,316.87	$2,771.52	$2,215.47	$1,961.66	$9,265.52

Basic Solutions

	Relevant	Irrelevant
The cost of a prior paint job, in a decision to repaint a building.		✓
The original investment cost in shares of stock in a company that is in decline, in a decision to sell or hold.		✓
Income taxes that can be saved by selling an asset at a loss, in a decision to sell or hold.	✓	
The cost of tearing out an old parking lot, in deciding whether or not to build a new lot.	✓	
The cost of textbooks, in deciding which classes to take during a semester.	✓	
The original cost of a textbook, in deciding whether or not to resell the book at the end of the term.		✓
The cost of an attorney, in deciding whether to appeal a traffic fine that is undeserved.	✓	
The allocation of factory depreciation, in deciding whether to accept a special offer from a customer.		✓
Research and development costs incurred to develop a new product, in deciding whether to file for a patent application.		✓
Proceeds that will be received from the sale of "factory seconds," in deciding how to price a primary product.	✓	

(a)

	Internal	Outsource
Direct materials	$ 50,000,000	$ 40,000,000
Direct labor	80,000,000	56,000,000
Variable factory overhead	16,000,000	12,000,000
Fixed factory overhead	35,000,000	35,000,000
Outsourced compressors (500,000 X $90)	-	45,000,000
Total cost of each option	$181,000,000	$188,000,000

It appears that it will cost more to outsource. Based on this quantitative analysis the company would not outsource the compressors.

(b)

	Outsource @ 600,000 units
Direct materials (600,000/500,000 X $40,000,000)	$ 48,000,000
Direct labor (600,000/500,000 X $56,000,000)	67,200,000
Variable factory overhead (600,000/500,000 X $12,000,000)	14,400,000
Fixed factory overhead	35,000,000
Outsourced compressors (600,000 X $90)	54,000,000
Total cost if 600,000 units are built	$218,600,000

Although costs increase by $37,600,000 ($218,600,000 - $181,000,000), revenues would increase far more (100,000 additional units X $600 each = $60,000,000). It seems that the company will be better off by outsourcing. The company would also want to consider nonquantitative factors such as quality of product and reliability of the supply chain.

(a)

Direct materials	$12.50
Direct labor	6.25
Variable factory overhead	18.75
Fixed factory overhead	25.00
Variable selling, general, and administrative costs	18.75
Fixed selling, general, and administrative costs	4.00
Total per unit cost @ 400,000 boxes	$85.25

The company needs to price the paintballs at $85.25 per box to cover all costs.

(b)

Accepting the special order will improve profitability. The variable costs are $56.25 ($12.50 + $6.25 + $18.75 + $18.75), and the order price of $75.00 per box has a per unit contribution margin of $18.75 ($75.00 - $56.25). Fixed costs will not change, thus overall profitability will significantly improve. Be sure to consider how capacity limitations and nonquantitative factors (such as the reaction of other customers paying $85.25 per box) might override this conclusion.

Below is an analysis reflecting the elimination of electronics. Jewelry sales and variable expenses of jewelry are each increased by 30%. The total fixed costs of $900,000 are distributed evenly to the two product lines.

Spreadsheet					□ ◻ ✕
		fx			
	A	B	C	D	E
1		Total	Beverages	Jewelry	~~Electronics~~
2	Sales	$2,050,000	$1,400,000	$650,000	$ -
3	Variable expenses	1,240,000	980,000	260,000	-
4	Contribution margin	$ 810,000	$420,000	$390,000	$ -
5	Fixed expenses	900,000	450,000	450,000	-
6	Income (loss)	$ (90,000)	$ (30,000)	$ (60,000)	$ -
7					

Note that eliminating electronics causes a sharp drop in profits. Even though Electronics appeared to result in a loss, its contribution margin was positive. The positive contribution margin helped to absorb fixed costs that cannot be avoided.

(a)

$$(1+i)^n$$

Where "i" is the interest rate per period and "n" is the number of periods

$$(1.05)^{10} = 1.628894627$$

$$1.628894627 \times \$1,000 = \$1,628.89$$

The 10-periods row, and 5% column factor is also 1.62889

(b)

$$(1.005)^{24} = 1.127159776$$

$$1.127159776 \times \$5,000 = \$5,635.80$$

The 24-periods row, and 0.50% column factor is also 1.12716

(c)

$$(1.05)^6 = 1.340095641$$

$$1.340095641 \times \$2,500 = \$3,350.24$$

The 6-periods row, and 5% column factor is also 1.34010

(d)

$$(1.02)^{20} = 1.485947396$$

$$1.485947396 \times \$7,500 = \$11,144.61$$

The 20-periods row, and 2% column factor is also 1.48595

(a)

$$(1+i)^n$$

Where "i" is the interest rate per period and "n" is the number of periods

Growth of first payment: $(1.08)^3$ X $1,000 = $1,259.71

Growth of second payment: $(1.08)^2$ X $1,000 = $1,166.40

Growth of third payment: $(1.08)^1$ X $1,000 = $1,080.00

$1,259.71 + $1,166.40 + $1,080.00 = $3,506.11

For an "annuity due," the 3-periods row, and 8% column factor is 3.50611

(b)

$$(1+i)^n$$

Where "i" is the interest rate per period and "n" is the number of periods

Growth of first payment: $(1.08)^2$ X $1,000 = $1,166.40

Growth of second payment: $(1.08)^1$ X $1,000 = $1,080.00

Growth of third payment: $(1.08)^0$ X $1,000 = $1,000.00

$1,166.40 + $1,080.00+ $1,000.00 = $3,246.40

For an "ordinary annuity," the 3-periods row, and 8% column factor is 3.24640

(c)

For an "annuity due," the 6-periods row, and 4% column factor is 6.89829

6.89829 X $500 = $3,449.15

(a)

$$1/(1+i)^n$$

Where "i" is the interest rate per period and "n" is the number of periods

$$(1.10)^{20} = 0.148643$$

$$0.148643 \times \$1,000,000 = \$148,643$$

The 20-periods row, and 10% column factor is also 0.14864

(b)

$$1/(1.005)^{24} = 0.887186$$

$$0.887186 \times \$5,000 = \$4,435.93$$

The 24-periods row, and 0.50% column factor is also 0.88719

(c)

$$1/(1.02)^{20} = 0.67297$$

$$0.67297 \times \$15,000 = \$10,094.57$$

The 20-periods row, and 2% column factor is also 0.67297

(d)

$$(1.06)^6 = 0.70496$$

$$0.70496 \times \$25,000 = \$17,624$$

The 6-periods row, and 6% column factor is also 0.70496

(a)

$$1/(1+i)^n$$

Where "i" is the interest rate per period and "n" is the number of periods

Present value of first payment: $1/(1.06)^1$ X $10,000 = $9,433.96

Present value of second payment: $1/(1.06)^2$ X $10,000 = $8,899.96

Present value of third payment: $1/(1.06)^3$ X $10,000 = $8,396.19

Present value of fourth payment: $1/(1.06)^4$ X $10,000 = $7,920.94

$9,433.96 + $8,899.96 + $8,396.19 + $7,920.94 = $34,651.05

For an "ordinary annuity," the 4-periods row, and 6% column factor is 3.46511

(b)

$$1/(1+i)^n$$

Where "i" is the interest rate per period and "n" is the number of periods

Present value of first payment: $1/(1.06)^0$ X $10,000 = $10,000.00

Present value of second payment: $1/(1.06)^1$ X $10,000 = $9,433.96

Present value of third payment: $1/(1.06)^2$ X $10,000 = $8,899.96

Present value of fourth payment: $1/(1.06)^3$ X $10,000 = $8,396.19

$10,000.00 + $9,433.96 + $8,899.96 + $8,396.19 = $36,730.11

For an "annuity due," the 4-periods row, and 6% column factor is 3.67301

(c)

For an "ordinary annuity," the 8-periods row, and 3% column factor is 7.01969

7.01969 X $5,000 = $35,098.45

(a)

	Cash Flow	X	Present Value Factor @ 8%	=	Present Value
Initial investment	$ (280,824)		1.00000		$ (280,824)
Annual cash flow	66,667		3.99271		266,182
Net present value					$ (14,642)

(b)

Annual increase in income = $66,667 - ($280,824/5 years) = $10,502.20

Annual increase in income ÷ investment = $10,502.20/$280,824 = 3.74%

(c)

	Cash Flow	X	Present Value Factor @ 6%	=	Present Value
Initial investment	$ (280,824)		1.00000		$ (280,824)
Annual cash flow	66,667		4.21236		280,824
Net present value					$ -

The internal rate of return is 6%.

(d)

Initial investment ÷ annual net cash inflows = $280,824/$66,667 = 4.21 years

Involved Solutions

Canyon City Proposal:

The staff proposal to close the store is incorrect. If the store is closed, the company will still incur $325,000 of fixed costs. This loss will exceed the $250,000 loss that is currently being experienced. At present, the store has sufficient contribution margin to cover the avoidable fixed costs and a portion of the unavoidable fixed costs.

Outsource Onions Proposal:

The potential to rent the farm to another is a relevant factor to consider. The $2,200,000 proposed purchase price, less $350,000 of rental income, is less than the current growing cost of $2,000,000. The staff proposal is again faulty.

Sell Packaged Beef Proposal:

The company would be better off to sell packaged beef. The $4 price exceeds the variable costs. The fixed costs are not relevant to this decision since they will be incurred in any event. The staff's logic is incorrect.

Scrap Packaging Material Proposal:

The unneeded material should be scrapped. The company will save $2,000 per year. The impact on income is not relevant since it is only an accounting outcome at this point (not an economic factor), and should likely occur whether or not the material is physically destroyed or not (Instructor Note: You might mention that a tax benefit could result at the time of physical destruction of the inventory, but not before). The staff again applied faulty logic.

Various present/future values calculations *I-24.02*

	Case A	Case B	Case C	Case D	Case E	Case F
Type	Ordinary annuity	Annuity due	Lump sum	Ordinary annuity	Lump sum	Annuity due
Sequence	End of period	Beginning of period	n/a	End of period	n/a	Beginning of period
Present value	$1,580	$13,484	$25,000	$12,746	$7,107	$23,354
Future value	$2,114	$17,100	$31,743	$16,184	$10,000	$24,794
Payment	$375 per year	$1,250 per quarter	n/a	$600 per quarter	n/a	$2,000 per month
Annual rate	6%	8%	12%	4%	5%	6%
Compounding	Annually	Quarterly	Monthly	Quarterly	Annually	Monthly
Duration	5 years	3 years	2 years	6 years	7 years	1 year

The present value (at 12%) of the expected cash inflows is $277,794, as calculated below. This exceeds the initial investment of $250,000 by $27,794, producing a positive net present value. The investment will return in excess of 12%, if it delivers as promised. However, there is a risk the investment will fail, and this should be considered in setting the targeted rate of return.

	Amount	Present Value Factor @ 12%	Present Value
Return at end of Year 1	$ -	0.89286	$ -
Return at end of Year 2	-	0.79719	-
Return at end of Year 3	40,000	0.71178	28,471
Return at end of Year 4	40,000	0.63552	25,421
Return at end of Year 5	40,000	0.56743	22,697
Return at end of Year 6	40,000	0.50663	20,265
Return at end of Year 7	400,000	0.45235	180,940
Total present value			$277,794

Net Present Value

	Amount	Ordinary Annuity Present Value Factor @ 8%	Present Value	Net Present Value (PV - $50,000)
Chipper (3)	$18,360	2.57710	$47,316	$ (2,684)
Truck (5)	12,195	3.99271	48,691	(1,309)
Grinder (7)	9,935	5.20637	51,725	1,725
Lift rig (9)	6,422	6.24689	40,118	(9,882)

Internal Rate of Return

	Amount	Ordinary Annuity Present Value Factor @ X%	Present Value	IRR (X%)
Chipper (3)	$18,360	2.72325	$49,999	**5%**
Truck (5)	12,195	4.10020	50,002	**7%**
Grinder (7)	9,935	5.03295	50,002	**9%**
Lift rig (9)	6,422	7.78611	50,002	**3%**

Accounting Rate of Return

	Amount	Depreciation (cost/life)	Annual increment to income	Incremental income ÷ $50,000
Chipper (3)	$18,360	$16,667	$1,693	**3.39%**
Truck (5)	12,195	10,000	2,195	**4.39%**
Grinder (7)	9,935	7,143	2,792	**5.58%**
Lift rig (9)	6,422	5,556	866	**1.73%**

Payback

	Amount	Annual cash flow ÷ $50,000
Chipper (3)	$18,360	2.72
Truck (5)	12,195	4.10
Grinder (7)	9,935	5.03
Lift rig (9)	6,422	7.79

	Income	Cash flows
Annual net revenue	$1,000,000	$1,000,000
Less: Depreciation	700,000	
Income before tax	$ 300,000	
Income tax (35%)	105,000	105,000
Net income	$ 195,000	$ 895,000

$895,000 per year, discounted for 5 years at 7%, has a present value of $3,669,679 ($895,000 X 4.10020). This exceeds the $3,500,000 investment by $169,679, and therefore has a positive net present value.

Photo Credits

Cover
TB Studio/Shutterstock.com

Made in United States
Orlando, FL
03 April 2023

31676270R00076